SOPHIE KOOKS

Sophie Kooks

QUICK AND EASY FEELGOOD FOOD

SOPHIE MORRIS

GILL & MACMILLAN

GILL & MACMILLAN
Hume Avenue, Park West, Dublin 12
with associated companies throughout the world
www.gillmacmillanbooks.ie

© Sophie Morris 2012
978 07171 5440 1

Design and print origination by www.grahamthew.com
Photography by Joanne Murphy
Styled by Orla Neligan
Assistant to photographer and stylist: Carly Horan

PROPS SUPPLIED BY:
AVOCA: H/O, Kilmacanogue, Bray, Co. Wicklow.
T: (01) 286 7466; E: info@avoca.ie; W: www.avoca.ie.

EDEN HOME & GARDEN: 1-4 Temple Grove, Temple Road, Blackrock, Co. Dublin.
T: (01) 764 2004; E: edenhomeandgarden@hotmail.com; W: www.edenhomeandgarden.ie.

MEADOWS & BYRNE: Dublin, Cork, Galway, Clare, Tipperary.
T: (01) 280 5444/(021) 434 4100; E: info@meadowsandbyrne.com;
W: www.meadowsandbyrne.com.

ARTICLE: Powerscourt Townhouse, South William Street, Dublin 2.
T: (01) 679 9268; E: items@articledublin.com; W: www.articledublin.com.

ELIZABELLE: 23 Church Street, Listowel, Co. Kerry.
T: (068) 22593; W: www.elizabelle.com.

MARKS & SPENCER: Unit 1-28, Dundrum Town Centre, Dublin 16.
T: (01) 299 1300; W: www.marksandspencer.ie.

CATH KIDSTON: Level 1 Unit 49, Dundrum Town Centre, Dublin 16.
T: (01) 296 4430; E: dundrum@cathkidston.co.uk; W: www.cathkidston.co.uk.

Index compiled by Cover to Cover
Printed by Printer Trento Srl, Italy
This book is typeset in 10 point Archer book on 12.

The paper used in this book comes from the wood pulp of managed forests. For every tree
felled, at least one tree is planted, thereby renewing natural resources.

A CIP catalogue record for this book is available from the British Library.

1 3 5 4 2

DEDICATION

This book is dedicated to my
mum Shelagh and my dad Tim.
You are both the best.

With tonnes of love,
Soph

CONTENTS

ACKNOWLEDGMENTS

Making this book has been a real dream come true and I want to send big thanks to the people who helped me get here.

My first and biggest thank you is to Graham, my Kooky Dough partner in crime! Thank you for believing in me from the very beginning, for pushing me when I doubted myself and for supporting me in every way imaginable. I couldn't have done this without you. Plus the book wouldn't be the same without your courgette-grilling skills!

Next, I would like to say a massive thank you to Nicki Howard from Gill & Macmillan. This book would not have happened without you and I will always be truly grateful. Thank you for believing in me.

Big thanks to the amazing food photography trio – Jo, Orla and Carly. I can't thank you enough for making my food come to life in such a beautiful way. It was such a pleasure working with you gorgeous ladies!

Thank you to the whole team at Gill & Macmillan who have made this book so special. To D Rennison Kunz, Emma Farrell, Teresa Daly and Ciara O'Connor – thank you for truly believing in the sentiment of this book.

Thank you to Graham Thew who hit the nail on the head with the design – I am so chuffed with how fantastic every page looks.

Thanks to Aisling Walsh, our genius Kooky Dough designer and a great friend. Your creativity astounds me; thank you so much for all your guidance and for always going above and beyond!

A big thank you to my gorgeous friend Nikki, and McDowell's Jewellers, for lending me your beautiful jewellery and making me feel so elegant!

Thank you to Bernie for all the supportive chats and for helping me in the food photography shoot; you are just great.

Thanks to Darina Allen and everyone at Ballymaloe Cookery School, where I first got the inspiration to have a food business one day.

To my amazing friends in Ireland and London, and the ones who've fled further afield – you know who you are... I love you all and come home soon!!

Thank you so much, Dad, for always being so supportive and encouraging, so generous, and a mountain of wisdom in my life. I admire you greatly.

And thank you Amanda for letting me take over your fabulous apartment – I'll never forget it.

To my lovely brother Ru and the rest of my family, both in South Africa and Ireland; you mean the world.

And lastly – thank you, Mum, for being so kind, so selfless in everything you do, and so fantastic in your mad, unique way! I miss you every day but I'm so happy to see you so happy, and I know you're always here for me. This book is for you...

Sophie

INTRODUCTION

Hello! I'm Sophie, owner of Irish food company Kooky Dough. Before starting Kooky Dough with my business partner Graham in 2009, I had no experience of working in the food industry at all, but it had been my dream for a long time to have a food business.

My interest in food began as a young girl, watching my mum buzz about frantically in the kitchen. It amazed me every time, after all her fretting, she would produce incredibly beautiful food. I guess she just didn't know how good a cook she was. I wanted to be like her – minus the frantic part, of course. So I started to cook a lot during college when I moved out of home. I became obsessed with trying new things and I loved cooking for friends. My eagerness to learn more led me to the Ballymaloe Cookery School in 2008. I adored the experience and it was then that I started to really think about having my own food business one day.

Of course, I have to admit that I chickened out completely when I moved back to Dublin! I took a financial services job based on my college qualifications. I knew I'd done the wrong thing as soon as I started, but it was 2008 – a scary time to be looking for a job in Ireland. Despite this (and despite numerous people telling me I was crazy), I quit the job quite quickly to pursue a career in food. Before long, Graham and I were standing behind a fold-up table in the farmers' market in Stillorgan selling rolls of cookie dough that we'd made in my tiny mixer at home. And the rest, as they say, is history…

We're incredibly fortunate that Kooky Dough has gone so well for us so far and although it's extremely hard work running a young business, it's still very exciting and full of surprises! One thing I've always been adamant about throughout all the crazy, long working days we've had, is to eat well every night and to keep cooking from scratch. I really do believe it's the key to staying on top of a hectic life! Not only does cooking help me unwind in the evening time, it keeps me healthy and I'm also positive it keeps my concentration and energy levels up.

I have a lot of friends who work crazy hours and have lives just as hectic as mine, but they're at a loss in the evenings as to what to cook. They want something that won't take too long or too much effort, so they end up having things like beans on toast – not very inspiring five days a week... This is how I got the idea for the book. I wanted to write down all the things that I manage to cook during my manic week; things that aren't too tiring or complicated. With some very basic store cupboard essentials and a weekly fresh food shop, you'll be laughing!

The book is broken into chapters by month, so dip into the book at whatever month you're in and you'll find lots of ideas for what to cook. Of course, feel free to break the rules and try any recipe that takes your fancy whatever the time of year. And the most important thing is to have fun cooking!

I hope you all enjoy the recipes as much as I do.

Love,

Sophie x

 Of course, I wouldn't be me if I didn't throw in a load of recipes for yummy baked goodies and desserts. Life would be no fun if we didn't treat ourselves!

GOOD-TO-HAVES

LARDER

olive oil

butter

eggs

cream

salt and black peppercorns

lemons

limes

onions

garlic

ginger

chillies

potatoes

nuts (almonds, hazelnuts, peanuts, pecans)

honey

pasta

rice

couscous

egg noodles

porridge oats

canned beans (butterbeans, cannellini, chickpeas)

canned tomatoes

lentils

stock cubes

red and white wine

chilli powder

dried chillies or chilli flakes

cayenne pepper

paprika

curry powder

curry pastes

dried oregano or dried thyme

soy sauce

sweet chilli sauce

balsamic vinegar

red or white wine vinegar

wholegrain mustard

Dijon mustard

caster sugar

brown sugar

icing sugar

flour

self-raising flour

baking powder

bread soda (bicarbonate of soda)

cocoa powder

vanilla extract

golden syrup

chocolate

GOOD-TO-HAVES

EQUIPMENT

good knives
chopping board
saucepans
frying pan or grill pan
ovenproof dishes
mixing bowls
food processor
electric whisk (handheld or free-standing)
grater
colander
wooden spoon
slotted spoon
potato masher
spatula
balloon whisk
sieve
baking sheets
cake tins (loaf tin, muffin tin)
rolling pin
kitchen towel
cling film
tin foil
parchment paper

KOOKSPEAK

I DON'T BELIEVE IN FUSSING IN THE KITCHEN – AND YOU'LL NOTICE THAT SOMETIMES I DON'T USE PRECISE MEASUREMENTS IN RECIPES. IF YOU SEE 'A LUG OF OLIVE OIL', IT MEANS AROUND A TABLESPOON (15 ML). THE SAME GOES FOR 'A KNOB OF BUTTER'. THE POINT IS NOT TO WORRY ABOUT THESE THINGS. JUST GO WITH YOUR INSTINCTS AND HAVE FUN!

WHAT'S WOW NOW!

Every fruit and vegetable has a seasonal time when it is at its very best. When in season, fruits and vegetables are super-fresh and have extra flavour. They also tend to be great value in the shops, since they're sourced locally rather than being flown in from thousands of miles away.

Some fruits and vegetables are great the whole year round; others are in season for just a month or two. Use the guide below to help you shop more seasonably.

JANUARY

BEETROOT, BROCCOLI (PURPLE SPROUTING), BRUSSELS SPROUTS, CABBAGE, CARROTS, CAULIFLOWER, CELERIAC, KALE, LEEKS, MUSHROOMS, PARSNIPS, SWEDES, TURNIPS

MARCH

BROCCOLI (PURPLE SPROUTING), BRUSSELS SPROUTS, CABBAGE, CARROTS, CAULIFLOWER, KALE, LEEKS, MUSHROOMS, PARSNIPS, SCALLIONS, SWEDES

MAY

ASPARAGUS, AUBERGINES, CABBAGE, CAULIFLOWER, CUCUMBERS, MUSHROOMS, PEPPERS, RADISH, RHUBARB, SCALLIONS, SPINACH, TOMATOES

FEBRUARY

BEETROOT, BROCCOLI (PURPLE SPROUTING), BRUSSELS SPROUTS, CABBAGE, CARROTS, CAULIFLOWER, CELERIAC, KALE, LEEKS, MUSHROOMS, PARSNIPS, SWEDES

APRIL

CABBAGE, CAULIFLOWER, MUSHROOMS, RHUBARB, SCALLIONS

JUNE

ASPARAGUS, AUBERGINES, BEETROOT, BLACKCURRANTS, BROAD BEANS, BROCCOLI (GREEN), CABBAGE, CAULIFLOWER, COURGETTES, CUCUMBERS, FRENCH BEANS, MUSHROOMS, POTATOES (NEW SEASON), PEPPERS, RADISH, RHUBARB, SCALLIONS, SHALLOTS, SPINACH, STRAWBERRIES, TOMATOES, TURNIPS

JULY

AUBERGINES, BEETROOT, BLACKBERRIES, BROAD BEANS, BROCCOLI (GREEN), CABBAGE, CARROTS, CAULIFLOWER, CELERY, CHERRIES, COURGETTES, CUCUMBERS, FRENCH BEANS, GOOSEBERRIES, MUSHROOMS, POTATOES (NEW SEASON), PEAS, PEPPERS, RADISH, RASPBERRIES, RHUBARB, RUNNER BEANS, SCALLIONS, SHALLOTS, SPINACH, STRAWBERRIES, TOMATOES, TURNIPS

SEPTEMBER

APPLES, BEETROOT, BLACKBERRIES, BROCCOLI (GREEN), BRUSSELS SPROUTS, BUTTERNUT SQUASH, CABBAGE, CARROTS, CAULIFLOWER, CELERY, COURGETTES, CUCUMBERS, FRENCH BEANS, KALE, LEEKS, MUSHROOMS, ONIONS, PARSNIPS, PEAS, PEPPERS, PLUMS, POTATOES (MAIN CROP), RADISH, RASPBERRIES, RHUBARB, RUNNER BEANS, SPINACH, STRAWBERRIES, SWEDES, SWEETCORN, TOMATOES, TURNIPS

NOVEMBER

BEETROOT, BROCCOLI (GREEN), BROCCOLI (PURPLE SPROUTING), BRUSSELS SPROUTS, BUTTERNUT SQUASH, CABBAGE, CARROTS, CAULIFLOWER, CELERIAC, CELERY, KALE, LEEKS, MUSHROOMS, PARSNIPS, PEARS, POTATOES (MAIN CROP), PUMPKINS, SWEDES, TURNIPS

AUGUST

AUBERGINES, BEETROOT, BLACKBERRIES, BLUEBERRIES, BROAD BEANS, BROCCOLI (GREEN), CABBAGE, CARROTS, CAULIFLOWER, CELERY, COURGETTES, CUCUMBERS, FRENCH BEANS, MUSHROOMS, ONIONS, PARSNIPS, PEAS, PEPPERS, PLUMS, RADISH, RASPBERRIES, RHUBARB, RUNNER BEANS, SCALLIONS, SHALLOTS, SPINACH, STRAWBERRIES, SWEDES, SWEETCORN, TOMATOES, TURNIPS

OCTOBER

APPLES, BEETROOT, BROCCOLI (GREEN), BRUSSELS SPROUTS, BUTTERNUT SQUASH, CABBAGE, CARROTS, CAULIFLOWER, CELERIAC, CELERY, KALE, LEEKS, MUSHROOMS, ONIONS, PARSNIPS, PEARS, PEPPERS, POTATOES (MAIN CROP), PUMPKINS, RADISH, RASPBERRIES, SCALLIONS, SPINACH, STRAWBERRIES, SWEDES, TOMATOES, TURNIPS

DECEMBER

BEETROOT, BROCCOLI (PURPLE SPROUTING), BRUSSELS SPROUTS, CABBAGE, CARROTS, CAULIFLOWER, CELERIAC, KALE, LEEKS, MUSHROOMS, PARSNIPS, PEARS, PUMPKINS, SWEDES, TURNIPS

JAN UARY

CHRISTMAS HAS PASSED, WE'VE HAD A GREAT TIME OVER-INDULGING AND THERE'S PROBABLY HALF A TURKEY STILL LEFT IN THE FRIDGE! JANUARY ISN'T SEEN AS THE MOST FUN MONTH – WE TEND TO TRY AND JUST GET THROUGH IT – BUT IT CAN BE A CHANCE TO CATCH YOUR BREATH AFTER THE CRAZINESS OF CHRISTMAS, CURL UP IN FRONT OF THE FIRE AND ENJOY THE SIMPLE PLEASURES OF COMFORTING, WHOLESOME AND DELICIOUS FOOD.

SPICED PARSNIP AND CARROT SOUP

After all the indulgence at Christmas, soup can be a welcome relief. This particular soup can make a wonderful meal to calm the tummy after too much turkey and all the trimmings. It's also a great way to use up leftover winter vegetables, so feel free to experiment! **Serves 4–6**

butter
1 leek, finely sliced
1 garlic clove, crushed
2 large parsnips, scrubbed and cubed
2 large carrots, scrubbed and cubed
salt and freshly ground black pepper
1 tablespoon plain flour
1 tablespoon curry powder
1 litre chicken or vegetable stock, simmering
100 ml milk or cream (optional)

1 Melt a knob of butter in a large saucepan and add the leek, garlic, parsnips and carrots. Season and stir well. Cover and cook over a low heat for 10 minutes, until soft.

2 Stir in the flour and curry powder and gradually incorporate the stock, stirring all the time. Simmer uncovered for 10–15 minutes, until the vegetables are fully cooked.

3 Purée with a hand blender until completely smooth. Add the milk or cream, if using. Gently heat through and season to taste. To serve, ladle into warmed bowls.

TURKEY AND SMOKY BACON SALAD

My family cooks such a huge turkey at Christmas that we often have leftovers a week later. This salad is great for those days when you don't feel like spending a lot of time cooking and you want something quick and easy. It's a great way to use up turkey leftovers, but it also works really well with cooked chicken. **Serves 4**

balsamic vinegar (minimum 1 cup, but you can use more to make a larger quantity of syrup)
olive oil
6 slices smoky bacon, cut into thin strips
2 red onions, peeled and chopped into bite-sized pieces
a handful of pine nuts (optional)
a few handfuls of cooked turkey or chicken, cut into thin strips
4 handfuls of rocket or other nice salad leaves
Parmesan shavings (optional)

1 Pour the balsamic vinegar into a small saucepan. Simmer over a low heat, until it has reduced by half. It should be thick and syrupy, but be careful not to reduce it too much. You can make a big batch of syrup, as it will keep well in a bottle or jam jar in the fridge. It will last a few months and can be really handy for drizzling over salads or grilled meats.

2 Heat a little olive oil in a frying pan over a medium heat and fry the bacon strips. When they're crisp and golden, remove them from the pan with a slotted spoon and set aside. Add the onions and pine nuts to the bacon fat in the pan. Fry for about 10 minutes, stirring regularly, until the onions are caramelised. Add the turkey to the pan and toss around to warm through. Put the bacon back into the pan and mix well.

3 Pour everything from the pan into a large mixing bowl, add the rocket and toss well to combine. Divide the salad onto serving plates, giving each portion a generous drizzle of balsamic syrup. You can use a potato peeler to make Parmesan shavings to put on top of the salad. Serve immediately.

CHICKEN WITH PARMA HAM, MOZZARELLA AND ROAST LEEKS

This is a really nice way to liven up some chicken breasts with minimal effort. The leeks are a great accompaniment and can be used in lots of other meals.

I find this dish filling enough just as it is, but when I'm feeling in need of some carbs, I serve it with steamed baby potatoes and butter. **Serves 4**

For the leeks
4 leeks, washed, trimmed and sliced into 1 cm rounds
1 teaspoon thyme leaves, fresh or dried
½ glass white wine (optional)
butter
salt and freshly ground pepper

4 chicken breasts
4 slices Parma ham
4 slices mozzarella (preferably buffalo)

1 Preheat the oven to 200°C/400°F/gas 6. Put the leeks in an ovenproof dish and scatter the thyme leaves on top. Pour in the wine, if using. Dot a few knobs of butter over the leeks and season. Cover the dish with tin foil and bake for 25–30 minutes, until the leeks are soft and tender.

2 As soon as the leeks are in the oven, you can prepare the chicken for roasting. Wrap each chicken breast with a slice of Parma ham and arrange in another ovenproof dish. Once the leeks have had about 5 minutes in the oven, place the chicken breasts in the oven also.

3 Roast the chicken breasts for 15 minutes, then take them out of the oven and top each breast with a slice of mozzarella. Return the chicken to the oven for a further 7 minutes, until the chicken is cooked through and the mozzarella is nicely melted.

4 To serve, arrange each chicken breast on a warmed plate with a nice helping of soft leeks.

APPLE AND PECAN CRUMBLE PIE

I love the comfort of pies and crumbles during the winter months and they can be so simple to make. When time is limited, ready-made pastry offers a great shortcut. The pecan crumble topping in this pie is a nice twist on tradition. The pie keeps for 4–5 days, so it can be enjoyed after dinner throughout the week. Serves 8

500 g ready-made shortcrust pastry, thawed if frozen
6 eating apples, preferably Golden Delicious
85 g plain flour, plus extra for dusting
85 g butter, cold, plus extra for greasing
170 g brown or granulated sugar
¹/₂ teaspoon cinnamon (optional)
85 g pecan nuts, roughly chopped

1 Preheat the oven to 180°C/350°F/gas 4.

2 Roll out the pastry to 5 mm thickness on a lightly floured board and use it to line a buttered 25.5 cm (10 inch) tart tin with removable base. Prick the pastry with a fork. Line the pastry case with greaseproof paper and fill to the top with baking beans or dried pulses. Bake for 15 minutes, then remove from the oven. Carefully remove the beans and greaseproof paper. Brush the pastry case with some beaten egg and return it to the oven to bake for a further 5 minutes, until golden.

3 Meanwhile, peel and chop the apples into 2 cm cubes. For the crumble, simply place the flour, butter, sugar and cinnamon in a food processor and blitz until it resembles breadcrumbs. Then add the pecans and blitz again, until they are quite finely chopped but still have a few chunky pieces left.

4 Fill the baked pastry shell with the apples and sprinkle the crumble over the top, ensuring the apples are completely covered. Increase the oven temperature to 190°C/375°F/gas 5 and bake the pie for 35–40 minutes, until the topping is golden and the apple feels soft when a skewer is inserted.

5 Serve warm or cold with cream or vanilla ice cream.

ROASTED RED PEPPER, CARROT AND FETA DIP

This is a favourite amongst my friends and is often requested when I'm having them over for chats and nibbles. This recipe makes quite a large batch and any leftovers will last in the fridge for about a week, which is great for snacks – although it's so addictive it never lasts that long in my fridge!

It's yummy with toasted pitta bread, crackers, carrot sticks or red pepper strips.

3 red peppers, whole
5 carrots, scrubbed and left whole
200 g feta, cubed
50–100 ml olive oil, plus more for roasting the vegetables
salt and freshly ground pepper

1 Preheat the oven to 200°C/400°F/gas 6. Rub the red peppers and carrots lightly with olive oil and place them in an ovenproof dish. Roast for 30–45 minutes, until the carrots are tender when pierced with a knife and the skins of the peppers are blackened.

2 Put the peppers in a bowl, cover the bowl with cling film and leave them to cool. The steam in the bowl will help to make the peppers easier to peel. After 15 minutes, carefully peel the skin off the peppers using your fingers. Ensure that you do not rinse the peppers or discard any of the lovely juices that have formed at the bottom of the bowl – this will add great flavour to the dip. Remove the stalks, cores and seeds from the peppers.

3 Roughly chop the carrots and tip them into a food processor along with the peppers, their juices, and the feta. Turn on the processor and, while everything is blending, slowly pour in the olive oil. Check the mixture as you go – and stop adding the olive oil when you're happy with the consistency. Season to taste. If you feel the dip is too thick, you can always add more olive oil.

4 Serve in a nice big bowl, alongside carrot sticks, pitta bread or anything else that takes your fancy. Best served chilled.

PORK CHOPS WITH APPLES AND MUSTARD MASH

This dish is a really simple way of serving pork and apples, a classic combination! I like mustard mash with the chops but you can make whatever potatoes you like as an accompaniment. **Serves 4**

For the mash
1.2 kg floury potatoes, such as Maris Piper, peeled and halved
50 g butter
50 ml milk
2–3 tablespoons wholegrain mustard, according to your liking

4–6 pork chops, depending on their size and how hungry you are
salt and freshly ground black pepper
olive oil
2–4 eating apples, each cut into 10 slices
butter

1 Place the potatoes in a large saucepan with just enough cold water to cover them. Add a pinch of salt and bring to the boil. Boil for 15–20 minutes, until the potatoes are tender and easily broken with a fork. Drain them in a colander and leave for 2–3 minutes, until the steam has evaporated. (Always drain potatoes really well or you'll end up with watery mash.) Put the drained potatoes back into the dry saucepan and mash thoroughly with a potato masher. The harder you work the mash, the fluffier it will become! Once the lumps are gone, add the butter and mash again. Add the milk and mustard, stirring until combined. Season to taste.

2 While the potatoes are boiling, prepare the pork chops. Lay them on a chopping board and make shallow cuts at 1 cm intervals along the fat side of the chops. This will ensure they crisp up nicely when cooked. Season both sides of each chop.

3 Heat a few lugs of olive oil in a large frying pan over a medium-high heat. Cook the chops for 3 minutes on each side, until golden. Remove the chops from the pan and set aside. Add the apple slices and a knob of butter to the pan and fry for 2–3 minutes, until golden. Return the chops to the pan and cook them with the apples, turning them once, for another 2–3 minutes, until fully cooked.

4 To serve, place a chop (or two) on each plate, pour over the golden apples and their juices, and add a portion of mustard mash to the side.

FLAPJACKS

My mum taught me how to bake when I was very young – and it was one of my favourite things to do in the afternoon after school. Flapjacks are a great intro to the world of baking because they're so simple. They were among the first things I learned to make; and I continue to make them because I just can't resist their buttery, oaty crunchiness with a huge mug of tea for added comfort!

Flapjacks provide a nice bit of sweetness after dinner and they're also good to snack on during the day. They will last well in a biscuit tin for about 5 days. ***Makes 12–16 flapjacks***

250 g butter, plus extra for greasing
120 g Demerara or dark brown sugar
2 tablespoons honey
500 g porridge oats
1 teaspoon salt

1 Preheat the oven to 180°C/350°F/gas 4. Grease a 27 ½ cm x 18 cm (11 inch x 7 inch) shallow baking tin.

2 Melt the butter, sugar and honey in a saucepan over a medium heat. Pour the melted ingredients into a large mixing bowl and add the oats and salt. Mix until fully combined.

3 Spoon the mixture evenly into the baking tin, smoothing the surface with the back of the spoon. Bake for 20 minutes, until nicely golden.

4 Cut into squares straight away and then leave to cool in the tin. Serve warm or cold with a huge mug of tea.

SIRLOIN STEAK WITH CHILLI BUTTER
AND ROAST BABY POTATOES

There's nothing better than a good steak – and they can be so quick to prepare. I love flavoured butters to smear onto grilled meat before serving; and this chilli butter is especially good on steak.
Serves 4

For the chilli butter
75 g butter
1 ½ teaspoons chilli powder
1 teaspoon Dijon mustard

1 kg new baby potatoes, halved
olive oil
salt and freshly ground black pepper
4 x 200 g sirloin steaks (about 2 cm thick), removed from the fridge 15 minutes before cooking

1 Beat the butter, chilli powder and mustard in a bowl, until smooth. Form the butter into a log shape, wrap in cling film and refrigerate until ready to use. Flavoured butter will keep in the fridge for a few weeks and it's a handy thing to have.

2 Preheat the oven to 200°C/400°F/gas 6. Cook the potatoes in a large pan of boiling salted water for 5–7 minutes. Drain in a colander and allow them to dry completely. Place the dry potatoes in a roasting dish. Pour in a lug of olive oil and shake the pan to coat the potatoes evenly. (Don't use too much oil or the potatoes won't crisp well in the oven.) Season and place in the oven for about 30 minutes, or until the potatoes are brown and crisp at the edges.

3 Meanwhile, heat a grill pan or frying pan over a medium-high heat. Lay the steaks on a chopping board and make shallow cuts at 2 cm intervals along the fat side of each steak. Sprinkle pepper on both sides of each steak, rub lightly with olive oil and, just before placing in the pan, sprinkle both sides with salt. Cooking times *for each side* will vary, depending on thickness of steaks. Use the following guidelines:

Rare: 2–3 minutes   **Medium rare: 3–4 minutes**
Medium: 4–5 minutes   **Well done: 5–6 minutes**

4 Once the steaks have been cooked for the desired length of time on each side, use a tongs to turn each steak upright. Cook each steak fat-side down for 3 minutes, until the fat becomes crisp. Transfer the steaks to a plate, cover with tin foil and allow to rest for 3 minutes.

5 Remove the chilli butter from the fridge and cut a slice for each steak. Serve the steaks with melting chilli butter on top, and roast potatoes and a green salad on the side.

FIRST OF FEBRUARY, FIRST OF SPRING! I LOVE THE FEELING OF THE EARLY DAYS OF SPRING WHEN YOU KNOW THE DAYS ARE GOING TO GET LONGER AND THE HARSHNESS OF THE WINTER AIR WILL SOON FADE. BUT I DON'T KID MYSELF: IT'S STILL VERY COLD AND I STILL TURN TO HEARTY FOOD LIKE SOUPS AND STEWS, AND THE ALL-IMPORTANT BAKED TREATS THAT SATISFY MY SWEET TOOTH. THE CHORIZO, BEAN AND CABBAGE STEW IN THIS MONTH IS MY GO-TO RECIPE WHEN I'M CRAVING A STEW AND NEED IT IN A HURRY. IT'S PURE GOLD!

FEBRUARY

PASTA AMATRICIANA

Pasta is a great midweek meal, since it's so quick to rustle up. This particular pasta dish is one of my absolute favourites: an old reliable when I'm too hungry to wait longer than 20 minutes for dinner!

I use penne for this dish but it is just as nice with spaghetti, fusilli or whatever type of pasta you like. **Serves 4**

olive oil
10 slices smoky bacon, cut into thin strips
4–6 dried chillies, finely chopped or 2 teaspoons chilli flakes
2 red onions, finely sliced
2 x 400 g cans chopped tomatoes
1 tablespoon chopped fresh parsley or 1 teaspoon dried oregano
salt and freshly ground pepper
400 g penne pasta
Parmesan, grated (optional)

1 Heat a lug of olive oil in a large pan over a high heat. Add the bacon and chillies and fry until the bacon pieces start to turn brown and crispy at the edges. Be patient: do not add anything else to the pan until the bacon reaches this point! Add the onions, frying until they start to caramelise. Add the tomatoes, herbs and some freshly ground black pepper and stir well. Turn the heat to low-medium and allow the sauce to reduce for about 5 minutes, which will intensify all the flavours.

2 Meanwhile, cook the penne in a large pan of boiling salted water, according to packet instructions. Always cook pasta in a large volume of water. The Italians say the water should be as salty as sea water, so use plenty of salt and you won't have to season after cooking. Cook the pasta until al dente (tender but firm to the bite).

3 Drain the pasta, keeping back a few tablespoons of the cooking water. Return the pasta to its pan and stir with the cooking water. This will help to loosen the pasta and retain the seasoning. Add the pasta to the pan with the sauce and stir well to combine.

4 Serve immediately in warmed bowls and garnish with grated Parmesan.

CHORIZO, BEAN AND CABBAGE STEW

This stew is pure comfort in a bowl – great for warming you up on a cold day. It's quick and easy, so it makes a perfect midweek dinner. Everyone who tries it just loves it!

If you can't find chorizo sausages, good-quality pork sausages work well. It's always worth buying chorizo, though. It's one of my favourite ingredients. So much so that I find it hard not to munch slices of it when I'm preparing it for cooking...

*Tinned beans are another kitchen essential. They're economical, nutritious and a great addition to soups and stews. This stew is really versatile, so experiment with different combinations of beans. You can make the stew in a big batch and enjoy leftovers for a few days – the flavour often improves – or reduce the quantities if you'd like a smaller amount. **Serves 6***

olive oil
6 slices smoky bacon, cut into thin strips
225 g chorizo sausage, cut into I cm rounds
3 x 400 g cans chopped tomatoes
I litre chicken or vegetable stock, simmering
I head of Savoy cabbage
I x 400 g can butter beans, drained and rinsed
I x 400 g can cannellini beans, drained and rinsed
I x 400 g can chickpeas, drained and rinsed
I x 400 g can kidney beans, drained and rinsed
a handful of chopped fresh parsley
salt and freshly ground black pepper

1 Heat a few lugs of olive oil in a large casserole or pan over a high heat. (It needs to be a large pan for this recipe.) Fry the bacon for 3–4 minutes, until nicely browned. Add the chorizo and fry for another minute. Add the tomatoes and stock and simmer for 5 minutes.

2 Meanwhile, prepare the cabbage. Discard the tough outer leaves and cut the cabbage in half lengthways. Remove the core and cut the leaves crosswise into thin slices. Add the cabbage and drained beans to the stew and simmer for a further 7–10 minutes.

3 Add the parsley and season to taste. Serve in warmed bowls with thick slices of crusty bread on the side.

DARK CHOCOLATE AND ORANGE COOKIES

Part of my job at Kooky Dough is to come up with new flavours and products. As you can imagine, I've spent many years testing hundreds of different cookie recipes! The classic combination of chocolate and orange inspired this one.

Serve the cookies warm with vanilla ice cream for a yummy dessert. And remember you can always halve the recipe if you want fewer cookies. **Makes about 14 big cookies**

170 g butter, at room temperature
55 g caster sugar
220 g soft brown sugar
1 teaspoon vanilla extract
finely grated zest of 1 large orange
1 egg, beaten
250 g plain flour
1 teaspoon bread soda (bicarbonate of soda)
1/4 teaspoon salt
180 g dark chocolate, chopped into small chunks

1 Preheat the oven to 180°C/350°F/gas 4. Line two large baking sheets with parchment paper.

2 Cream the butter, sugars, vanilla and orange zest in a large bowl with an electric beater, until light and fluffy. Gradually beat in the egg until well combined.

3 Sift the flour, bread soda and salt into a medium bowl. With the mixer on low, slowly add the dry ingredients to the butter mixture. Mix until just combined. Stir in the chocolate chunks.

4 Drop level tablespoons of cookie dough onto the lined baking sheets, leaving lots of room between them so that they can spread out in the oven. Bake for 10–14 minutes, until golden around the edges but still soft in the centre. Leave to cool on the tray for a few minutes before serving warm, or transfer to a wire rack to cool further.

BAKED APPLES

The beauty of this healthy dessert is its simplicity – it is an absolute dream on a cold winter night. You can play around with different dried fruits and nuts in the filling, depending on what you have in your larder. **Serves 6**

6 eating apples
45 g sultanas
40 g soft brown sugar
20 g flaked almonds
$^3/_4$ teaspoon cinnamon
100 g butter, softened

1 Preheat the oven to 180°C/350°F/gas 4.

2 Use a paring knife to cut a small circle around the stem on the top of each apple. Cut down into the apple and remove the core, ensuring you leave about 1 cm of a base, so that the filling won't seep out during baking. Use a teaspoon to scoop out some of the apple flesh, creating a hole for the filling. Sit the apples snugly in an ovenproof dish. Place an equal amount of sultanas into each apple, pressing down firmly on the sultanas so that they reach the base.

3 Place the sugar, almonds, cinnamon and butter in a small bowl and mix well. Stuff as much of this mixture as you can into each apple. Smear the outside of each apple with the remaining mixture.

4 Bake the apples for 25–30 minutes, until they are golden and soft but not collapsing. Transfer the apples to individual serving bowls and spoon over the lovely juices that have formed at the bottom of the baking dish. These apples are yummy with crème fraîche, vanilla ice cream or softly whipped cream.

SPICY CHICKEN THIGHS WITH CANNELLINI BEANS

I find the dark meat of chicken thighs much tastier than the white meat of chicken breasts; and it's better value, too. The crispy skin of the chicken thighs and the spicy beans work really well together in this dish. The advantage of using tinned beans is that they're already cooked so they can be transformed quickly into a delicious midweek meal – a real winner in my book! **Serves 4**

8 chicken thighs (bone in, with skin)
salt and freshly ground black pepper
olive oil
2 green peppers, quartered
2 red peppers, quartered
1 red onion, roughly chopped
2 garlic cloves, peeled

2 red chillies, deseeded and roughly chopped
2 tablespoons paprika
juice of 2 lemons
6 tablespoons white wine vinegar
a handful of fresh coriander
2 x 400 g cans cannellini beans, drained and
  rinsed

1 Preheat the oven to 200°C/400°F/gas 6.

2 Heat a large frying pan over a high heat. Place the chicken thighs on a chopping board, skin side down, and slash the meat a few times with a sharp knife. Season both sides of the chicken thighs and rub with olive oil.

3 Rub the pepper strips with olive oil and place them skin side down in the hot frying pan. Leave them until the skins are blackened and they have softened, about 10 minutes.

4 Meanwhile, put the onions, garlic, chillies, paprika, lemon juice, vinegar and coriander into a food processor and blitz until smooth. Pour this spicy sauce into a large ovenproof dish and mix the cannellini beans into the sauce. Spread the mixture evenly around the dish.

5 When the peppers are ready, remove them from the pan and arrange them on top of the spicy bean mixture in the dish.

6 Now place the chicken thighs in the hot pan, skin side down. (It's important not to overcrowd the pan, so you might need to do this in batches.) Fry the thighs until the skins turn golden and crispy. Don't turn them too soon or the skin won't crisp up. The fat will render out of the chicken as it cooks; it can become very hot and spit out of the pan, so be careful. Once the skins are golden and crispy, turn the thighs over and cook for 5 minutes on the other side.

7 Place the chicken thighs, skin side up, on top of the peppers and beans. Don't coat the chicken with the sauce or the skins won't stay nice and crispy. Place the dish in the oven and roast for 15–20 minutes, until the chicken is fully cooked.

8 Serve with a simple green salad. Delish!

HERB-CRUSTED COD WITH PEPPER RATATOUILLE AND ROSEMARY CHIPS

Cooking fish midweek is great because you don't have to do that much to get lots of flavour and fish cooks very quickly. The Pepper Ratatouille and Rosemary Chips are lovely sides with this dish but you could serve the Herb-Crusted Cod with lots of things – mushy peas and chips would be yummy!
Serves 4

50 g butter
100 g breadcrumbs
1 tablespoon chopped fresh parsley
1 tablespoon fresh thyme leaves
4–5 large potatoes, such as Kerr's Pink, scrubbed and unpeeled
olive oil
1 tablespoon chopped fresh rosemary

salt and freshly ground black pepper
1 red onion, finely sliced
1 garlic clove, crushed
1 green pepper, sliced
1 red pepper, sliced
1 x 400 g can chopped tomatoes
sugar
4 x 180 g cod fillets, skinned and pinboned

1 Preheat the oven to 200°C/400°F/gas 6.

2 To prepare the herb crumbs, melt the butter in a small saucepan and stir in the breadcrumbs, parsley and thyme. Remove from the heat straight away and allow to cool.

3 For the chips, cut the potatoes lengthways into thick strips and dry them very well with kitchen paper or a clean tea towel. Place the potato strips in a large ovenproof dish, drizzle with a light coating of olive oil, sprinkle the rosemary on top, season and mix well to coat evenly. Roast for 25–30 minutes, until nicely browned.

4 As soon as the chips are in the oven, make the ratatouille. Heat a lug of olive oil in a medium saucepan over a low heat. Add the onion and garlic and cook gently, until softened but not browned. Add the peppers and fry for a few minutes, until softened. Add the tomatoes and stir well. Season and add a pinch of sugar to taste. Cover and simmer gently for about 20 minutes, until the peppers have softened but still hold their shape. Remove the lid for the final 5 minutes of cooking, to reduce the sauce a bit.

5 While the ratatouille is cooking, prepare the fish. It needs to go in the oven about 15 minutes after the potatoes. Season the cod fillets and roll them in the herb breadcrumbs. Press the crumbs against the flesh of the fish, covering both sides of each fillet. Place the fillets in an ovenproof dish and cook for 12–15 minutes (depending on thickness).

6 When the cod and chips are ready, remove them from the oven and divide them among warmed plates, alongside a nice helping of ratatouille.

LUCINDA'S LEMON DRIZZLE CAKE

My great friend Lu gave me this recipe when we were in college together and I haven't come across a better lemon cake recipe since. It's up there with my favourite simple cakes to bake and it's always a crowd-pleaser. Thanks, Lu! **Serves 8**

115 g butter, at room temperature, plus extra for greasing
175 g caster sugar
finely grated zest of 1 lemon
2 eggs, beaten
175 g self-raising flour
1 tablespoon poppy seeds (optional, but lovely)
4 tablespoons milk
120 g icing sugar
juice of 1 lemon

1 Preheat the oven to 180°C/350°F/gas 4. Grease a 900 g (2 lb) loaf tin and line it with parchment paper.

2 Cream the butter, sugar and lemon zest in a large bowl with an electric beater, until pale and fluffy. Gradually beat in the eggs until well combined. Sift the flour and poppy seeds into the bowl and mix until just incorporated. Add the milk and beat until the mixture loosens up and becomes really light and creamy. Pour the cake batter into the prepared loaf tin and bake for 30–40 minutes or until well risen in the centre. This cake should be quite moist, so a skewer inserted does not need to come out completely clean.

3 While the cake is in the oven, heat the icing sugar and lemon juice in a small pan over a low heat. Stir until all the sugar dissolves, remove from the heat and set aside.

4 When the cake is done, leave it in the tin and prick it quite deeply all over with a skewer. Pour the lemon sugar syrup over the cake so that the syrup sinks right down. Ideally, allow the cake to sit for 1–2 hours before eating.

5 If you like, you can frost the top of the cake with icing made by blending 220 g icing sugar with some lemon juice. Use the juice of half a lemon and add more if needs be, just enough to reach a stiff consistency.

6 The cake tastes even better the next day and will keep very well for 5–6 days in an airtight container. It is delicious served on its own, but really yummy with crème fraîche or vanilla ice cream.

TOMATO AND CHILLI SOUP WITH CRUNCHY CROUTONS

There's nothing better than a nice tomato soup – and once you taste a good homemade one, there's no going back to the tinned stuff!

I often like a bit of heat in soups, so that's why I include chilli here; but feel free to leave it out if you prefer. The croutons add a nice bit of texture and take away the need for a slice of bread on the side. And remember that soups freeze really well, so you can make a big batch of this one and freeze portions for reheating. **Serves 4 as a starter, 2 as lunch**

olive oil
I onion, finely chopped
I garlic clove, crushed
850 ml chicken or vegetable stock, simmering
I x 400 g can chopped tomatoes
I red chilli, deseeded and finely chopped (optional)
I tablespoon tomato purée
salt and freshly ground black pepper
I teaspoon sugar
a squeeze of lemon juice
2 slices white bread, cut into 2 cm cubes (preferably slightly stale)
a small handful of basil leaves (optional)

I Heat a lug of olive oil in a large saucepan over a medium heat. Add the onion and cook gently for about 10 minutes, until soft and translucent. Add the garlic and cook for another minute. Add the stock, tomatoes, chilli and tomato purée. Stir well and bring to the boil. Season, then add the sugar and lemon juice to taste. Reduce the heat and simmer uncovered for 20 minutes.

2 Meanwhile, make the croutons. Heat a few lugs of olive oil in a frying pan over a high heat, until a crumb sizzles vigorously when dropped in. Fry the bread in the hot oil for 1–2 minutes, until golden brown all over. Drain the croutons on kitchen paper to absorb the excess oil and sprinkle with a pinch of salt.

3 When the soup has finished simmering, stir in the basil leaves, if using. Purée with a hand blender until completely smooth. Gently heat through and season to taste, then ladle into warmed bowls and top with the crunchy croutons.

MARCH

ONLY IN MARCH DO I BEGIN TO FEEL THAT WINTER HAS FINALLY GONE. IT'S GREAT TO SEE THE BRIGHTER DAYS, TREES STARTING TO BLOOM AND NEW SPRING VEGETABLES POPPING UP. AS THE MONTH GOES ON, I SLOWLY MOVE AWAY FROM COMFORT FOOD TOWARDS LIGHTER DISHES LIKE PASTAS AND VIBRANT, FRESH CURRIES. I LOVE THIS TIME OF YEAR WITH ALL ITS PROMISE OF LONGER DAYS AND SUMMERTIME SOON TO COME...

LENTIL SHEPHERD'S PIE

My mum taught me this variation on traditional shepherd's pie years ago and it is absolutely delicious. I've cooked it for many people who were initially sceptical but later won over and in total agreement that you definitely don't miss the meat when eating it. Lentils are filling, nutritious and economical – a must-have for your store cupboard.

This pie freezes really well so you can make a big batch and keep the leftovers. And did I mention that my brother Ru likes to call it 'Leopard's Pie'? **Serves 4–6**

olive oil
2 onions, finely chopped
2 garlic cloves, crushed
2 carrots, grated
1 celery stick, finely chopped
400 g puy lentils, rinsed and drained (green or red lentils also work well)
1 x 400 g can chopped tomatoes
2 heaped tablespoons tomato purée
600 ml chicken or vegetable stock, simmering

1 teaspoon chilli powder or 1 teaspoon cayenne pepper
a sprig of thyme
salt and freshly ground black pepper

For the mash
1.2 kg floury potatoes, such as Maris Piper, peeled and halved
50 g butter
50 ml milk

1 Preheat the oven to 200°C/400°F/gas 6.

2 Heat a lug of olive oil in a large pan over a medium heat. Add the onions, garlic, carrots and celery and cook gently for about 10 minutes, until softened. Add the lentils, tomatoes, tomato purée, stock, chilli powder and thyme. Stir well and season. Bring to the boil, then reduce the heat and simmer for 40–50 minutes, until the lentils are softened. You may need to add more stock (or boiling water) throughout cooking if all the liquid is absorbed before the lentils are cooked.

3 Meanwhile, make the mash. Place the potatoes in a large saucepan with just enough cold water to cover them. Add a pinch of salt and bring to the boil. Boil for 15–20 minutes, until the potatoes are tender and easily broken with a fork. Drain them in a colander and leave for 2–3 minutes, until the steam has evaporated. (Always drain potatoes really well or you'll end up with watery mash.) Put the drained potatoes back into the dry saucepan and mash thoroughly with a potato masher. The harder you work the mash, the fluffier it will become! Once the lumps are gone, add the butter and mash again. Add the milk, stirring until combined. Season to taste.

4 Once the lentils are cooked, remove the sprig of thyme and pour the mixture into a deep ovenproof dish, leaving room for the mash topping. Arrange the mash evenly on top of the lentil mixture and bake the pie in the oven for 20 minutes or until nicely browned.

5 Serve on warmed plates, with a green salad on the side.

BUTTERSCOTCH BANANAS WITH VANILLA ICE CREAM

Bananas and butterscotch make an amazing combination and this gorgeous pudding is ready in less than 10 minutes. What could be better? Serves 6

6 ripe bananas, peeled and halved lengthways
a squeeze of lemon juice
60 g butter
50 g caster sugar
80 g soft brown sugar
130 g golden syrup
100 ml cream
¼ teaspoon vanilla extract (optional)
good vanilla ice cream

1 Place the bananas in a bowl, squeeze over some lemon juice and mix.

2 Melt the butter, sugars and golden syrup in a small saucepan over a low heat. Stir until completely combined, then continue to cook for 4–5 minutes. Gradually stir in the cream and vanilla extract, if using, and continue to cook for 2 minutes until the sauce is a lovely smooth consistency. Remove from the heat and allow to cool and thicken.

3 Place two big scoops of ice cream into each serving bowl. Divide the bananas among the serving bowls. Pour the butterscotch sauce over the bananas – and dig in! Any leftover butterscotch will keep for a few weeks in an airtight container in the fridge.

CLASSIC TAGLIATELLE RAGÙ

I've always loved the simplicity of Italian cooking: it's all about great flavours from the best-quality fresh ingredients. To celebrate my graduation from college, my mum and I went on holidays to a gorgeous hilltop village in Italy called Toffia, where we did a short Italian cookery course. There I learned a lot about the Italian way of cooking. I even took lessons from a 70-year-old lady who lived in the village. She had been making fresh pasta every day since she was a little girl and the only equipment she ever used was a large table and a giant rolling pin!

The sauce in this recipe is Bolognese sauce as we know it, though many Italians simply call it a ragù. It's a wonderful sauce for making lasagne, so it's worth doubling the recipe and freezing the leftovers for another day. I prefer tagliatelle with my ragù but you can use spaghetti or any other type of pasta. **Serves 4**

olive oil
2 onions, finely chopped
2 carrots, finely chopped
2 celery sticks, finely chopped
2 slices pancetta or streaky bacon, diced
450 g lean minced beef
100 ml red wine
2 x 400 g cans chopped tomatoes or 800 g passata (crushed, sieved tomatoes)
salt and freshly ground black pepper
450 g tagliatelle pasta
Parmesan, grated (optional)

1 Heat a few lugs of olive oil in a large pan over a medium-high heat. Fry the onion, carrot, celery and pancetta for about 10 minutes, until the pancetta is golden and the vegetables have softened. Add the mince and fry until golden brown. Turn up the heat, pour in the wine and let it evaporate for a few minutes. Add the tomatoes, season and stir well. Bring to the boil, reduce the heat and let the sauce simmer for at least 40 minutes (preferably 1 hour).

2 Cook the tagliatelle in a large pan of boiling salted water, according to packet instructions. Always cook pasta in a large volume of water. The Italians say the water should be as salty as sea water, so use plenty of salt and you won't have to season after cooking. Cook the pasta until al dente (tender but firm to the bite). Drain the pasta, keeping back a few tablespoons of the cooking water. Return the pasta to its pan and stir with the cooking water. This will help to loosen the pasta and retain the seasoning.

3 Add the Bolognese sauce to the cooked pasta and stir well to combine. Serve immediately in warmed bowls and garnish with grated Parmesan.

CHICKEN BALTI

Who doesn't love a good curry? I'm known to get very excited about curry nights with the whole works! A few curries, rice, naan bread, natural yogurt and a jar of mango chutney – that is just bliss for me.

I often spend an entire Sunday afternoon making a curry from scratch. It's not a very realistic option for a speedy midweek meal, though, so if I'm craving a curry and don't have much time, I use good-quality curry paste from the supermarket and a few core ingredients. Very little effort, but very big rewards. **Serves 4**

1 onion, roughly chopped
1 garlic clove
1 red chilli, deseeded and roughly chopped
a thumb-sized piece of ginger, peeled and roughly chopped
a handful of fresh coriander, leaves and stalks separated
olive oil
1 red pepper, roughly chopped
1 yellow pepper, roughly chopped
4 chicken breasts, cut into bite-sized pieces
140 g good-quality Balti curry paste (make sure it's not Balti curry sauce in a jar, it must be Balti paste!)
2 x 400 g cans chopped tomatoes
salt and freshly ground black pepper
a squeeze of lemon juice

1 Put the onion, garlic, chilli, ginger and coriander stalks (leave the coriander leaves aside for now) in a food processor and blitz until finely chopped. If the mixture doesn't chop easily, add a splash of water to loosen it.

2 Heat a few lugs of olive oil in a large pan over a medium-high heat. Add the mixture from the food processor into the pan and cook for about 10 minutes, until softened and lightly coloured. Add the peppers, chicken and Balti curry paste and mix well. Cook for a few minutes, before adding the tomatoes and about 100 ml of water. Stir well and bring to the boil. Reduce the heat and simmer the curry for 30 minutes. Season and add a good squeeze of lemon juice, to taste.

3 Serve the curry with boiled rice and garnish with coriander leaves. If you feel like going all out, buy some naan bread, natural yogurt and mango chutney to serve alongside.

Carrot cake is easily in my top 10 favourite cakes. It's the cake I often turn to when I get the urge for a baked treat. I've tried loads of recipes and this is by far the best one. I've used orange in the cream cheese icing here but sometimes I swap it for lemon, so go with whatever takes your fancy. The cake will keep well, covered in tin foil, for 4–5 days. **Makes a 23 cm round cake**

400 g soft brown sugar
4 eggs
340 ml sunflower oil
230 g plain flour
¹/₂ teaspoon salt
2 level teaspoons bread soda (bicarbonate of soda)
1 ¹/₂ teaspoons cinnamon
250 g carrots, grated
1 teaspoon vanilla extract
100 g walnuts, chopped

For the icing
125 g cream cheese
75 g butter, at room temperature
finely grated zest of 1 large orange
225 g icing sugar, sieved

1 Preheat the oven to 180°C/350°F/gas 4. Grease a deep 23 cm (9 inch) springform cake tin and line the base with parchment paper.

2 Whisk the sugar, eggs and oil in a large bowl with an electric beater, until smooth. Sift the flour, salt, bread soda and cinnamon into the bowl and mix well. Stir in the carrots, vanilla extract and walnuts and mix until combined. Pour the cake batter into the prepared tin and bake for 60–65 minutes or until a skewer inserted into the centre comes out clean. Leave to cool in the tin for about 10 minutes before turning out onto a wire rack to cool.

3 While the cake is cooling, make the icing. Beat the cream cheese, butter and orange zest in a small bowl with an electric beater. Sieve the icing sugar into the bowl and beat well. Place the bowl of icing in the fridge to set a bit while the cake is cooling.

4 Once the cake has cooled completely, spread the icing on top of the cake and allow it to drip down the sides. Serve slices of the cake with big mugs of tea.

MANGO LASSI

*A lassi is a traditional yogurt-based drink from India, which can be sweet or savoury. Mango lassi is very popular in India and it's sweet, just like a milkshake! It couldn't be easier to make and it tastes absolutely delicious after a curry. Sometimes lassis are spiced with cardamom but I've gone for a more basic recipe here, which is lovely. **Serves 4***

350 g Greek yogurt
100 ml milk
1 ½ tablespoons sugar
1 large ripe mango, peeled and roughly chopped

Place all the ingredients in a blender and blend for 1–2 minutes. Serve in individual glasses with or without ice. Simple!

CREAMY MUSHROOM CROSTINI

Crostini means 'little toasts' in Italian. They are a lovely starter or snack, consisting of small, grilled slices of bread with different toppings. This is a topping I particularly like. I sometimes have these crostini with a salad for dinner when I'm not too hungry. The great thing about crostini is the endless experimenting you can do with different toppings. **Serves 4**

butter
¹/₂ small onion, finely chopped
1 garlic clove, finely chopped
150 g mushrooms, sliced (button or flat)
1 teaspoon fresh thyme leaves
1 teaspoon finely grated lemon zest
salt and freshly ground black pepper
2 tablespoons crème fraîche
1 x French stick, cut into 2 cm rounds
olive oil

1 Preheat the oven to 180°C/350°F/gas 4.

2 Melt a knob of butter in a large frying pan over a medium heat. Add the onion and garlic and leave to sweat for a few minutes, until softened. Add the mushrooms in a single layer. (The rule for frying mushrooms is not to overcrowd the pan, so fry them in batches if you need to.) Add the thyme and lemon zest and season. Fry the mushrooms until they have released their juices, then add the crème fraîche. Stir well and allow to simmer for a few minutes.

3 For the crostini, drizzle the bread slices generously with olive oil and arrange on a baking sheet in a single layer. Place in the oven and bake for about 10 minutes, until golden brown and crispy.

4 When the bread is ready, top with the mushroom mixture and serve immediately.

LEMONY CHICKEN AND CHILLI PASTA

This is a super-quick, effortless pasta dish. It's a really handy one when you're tired and not in the mood to cook but you still want to be well fed! It takes just a handful of ingredients to make the sauce and, once the chicken is cooked, the meal comes together in a flash. I use linguine pasta but any shape will do. It's a surprisingly light dish – the perfect pick-me-up supper.
Serves 4

olive oil
4 chicken breasts, cut into thin strips
salt and freshly ground black pepper
2 red chillies, deseeded and finely chopped
a handful of chopped fresh parsley
200 g crème fraîche
juice of 1 lemon, divided
450–500 g linguine pasta

1 Heat a few lugs of olive oil in a frying pan over a medium heat. Add the chicken strips and season with salt and plenty of black pepper. Fry for a few minutes, then add the chillies and parsley. Fry for 5–7 minutes, until the chicken is fully cooked and golden. Add the crème fraîche and half the lemon juice and let the sauce simmer for a few minutes.

2 Meanwhile, cook the penne in a large pan of boiling salted water, according to packet instructions. Always cook pasta in a large volume of water. The Italians say the water should be as salty as sea water, so use plenty of salt and you won't have to season after cooking. Cook the pasta until al dente (tender but firm to the bite).

3 Drain the pasta, keeping back a few tablespoons of the cooking water. Return the pasta to its pan and stir with the cooking water. This will help to loosen the pasta and retain the seasoning. Add the chicken mixture to the cooked pasta and stir well to combine. Taste and add more lemon juice if needs be. Serve immediately in warmed bowls.

APRIL

WHEN I THINK OF APRIL, I THINK OF EASTER. I AM A CHOCOHOLIC SO IT'S ONE OF MY FAVOURITE TIMES OF YEAR – THE ONLY TIME WHEN I FEEL TRULY JUSTIFIED EATING COPIOUS AMOUNTS OF CHOCOLATE BARS AND BAKED TREATS. MALTEASTER ROCKY ROAD IS A STAPLE IN MY FRIDGE AROUND EASTERTIME, THOUGH I'LL ADMIT IT MAKES AN APPEARANCE AT OTHER TIMES OF THE YEAR, TOO. TRY IT AND YOU'LL SEE WHY!

EASY KOFTA CURRY

'Kofta' is the word for meatballs in the Middle East and South Asia. This beef kofta recipe with its warming curry sauce is a really simple one and so quick to prepare. Lamb kofta is also really nice, so you can swap the beef for minced lamb if you like. Serves 4–6

700 g lean minced beef
a thumb-sized piece of ginger, grated
3 garlic cloves, crushed
2 teaspoons chilli powder
salt and freshly ground pepper
olive oil
1 onion, finely chopped
600 ml passata (crushed, sieved tomatoes) or 2 x 400 g cans chopped tomatoes
2 heaped tablespoons medium curry powder (or mild, if you don't want much spice)
½ teaspoon sugar

1 Place the minced beef in a bowl along with the ginger, garlic and chilli powder. Season and mix with your hands until well combined. Roll the mixture into rounds about the size of golf balls and set aside.

2 Heat a few lugs of olive oil in a large pan over a medium heat. Fry the onion for 4–5 minutes, until softened. Add the passata, curry powder and sugar and bring to the boil. Reduce the heat, season and leave the sauce to simmer over a low heat while you fry the koftas.

3 Heat a few lugs of olive oil in a large frying pan. Fry the koftas for 2–3 minutes, turning them until lightly browned all over. (You might need to do this in batches.) Carefully place the cooked koftas into the passata sauce and simmer very gently for 15–20 minutes, turning the koftas occasionally during cooking, until they have set and the sauce has reduced nicely.

4 Serve on warmed plates with basmati rice and a dollop of natural yogurt.

MALTEASTER ROCKY ROAD

I have a real weakness for chocolate. After dinner, when I'm unwinding, I often get a craving for a chocolate fix – and this intensely chocolaty recipe really hits the spot. The Maltesers are a scrumptious addition; raisins or nuts are delicious, too. **Makes 16 squares**

300 g milk chocolate, roughly chopped
100 g dark chocolate, roughly chopped
100 g butter, cubed
3 tablespoons golden syrup
225 g Digestive biscuits
150 g mini marshmallows
135 g Maltesers

1 Line the base of a 20 cm (8 inch) square tin with parchment paper.

2 Place the chocolate, butter and golden syrup in a large heatproof bowl over a saucepan of simmering water. Make sure the bottom of the bowl doesn't touch the water. Don't stir until everything is nearly melted, then stir gently to bring it all together. Remove the bowl from the heat.

3 While the chocolate is melting, bash the Digestives into crumbs. You can put them in a Ziploc bag and bash them with a rolling pin or just break them with your hands. Place the Digestive crumbs and most of the marshmallows into a large bowl. Pour the melted chocolate mixture into the large bowl and stir to combine.

4 Pour the mixture into the lined baking tin. Sprinkle the Maltesers and remaining marshmallows over the top and, using the back of a wooden spoon, press them down into the mixture so they are lodged into place. Refrigerate for 1–2 hours to set, then cut into squares. Yum!

LAMB CHOPS WITH MINT SAUCE AND ROAST VEGETABLE COUSCOUS

I love the flavour of lamb; and lamb chops are perfect midweek, as they're super-quick to cook. There are so many things you can do with lamb chops but I've gone for the classic combo of lamb and mint because I find it irresistible!

Couscous is another must for the store cupboard. It's so easy to prepare that you can't go wrong. You might think couscous is bland but it really depends on what you do with it. It's so versatile; and the addition of herbs, spices or dried fruits can completely transform it. In this recipe, roast vegetables are mixed through the couscous along with a nice dressing. It makes a really yummy side dish for the lamb. Serves 4

For the couscous and dressing
1 red pepper, cut into eighths
1 yellow pepper, cut into eighths
1 sweet potato, peeled and cut into 4 cm pieces
1 courgette, cut into 4 cm pieces
1 red onion, cut into eighths
2 garlic cloves, unpeeled
olive oil
salt and freshly ground black pepper
200 g couscous
300 ml boiling water

a handful of flaked almonds (optional)
grated zest and juice of 1 lemon
a handful of finely chopped fresh mint

For the mint sauce
a handful of finely chopped fresh mint
1 tablespoon caster sugar
4 tablespoons white wine vinegar

8 lamb loin chops

1 Preheat the oven to 200°C/400°F/gas 6.

2 Place the peppers, sweet potato, courgette, onion and garlic cloves on a roasting tray. Add a lug of olive oil, season and mix well to coat evenly. Roast for 30–35 minutes, until the vegetables are completely soft.

3 Next, make the mint sauce. Put the mint, sugar, vinegar and 2 tablespoons of boiling water in a small bowl. Leave to infuse while everything is cooking.

4 Now toast the almond flakes, if using. Heat a small pan over a medium heat and add the almonds. Toast them for a few minutes, tossing regularly, until golden. Tip them into a bowl and set aside.

5 When the vegetables are in the oven about 20 minutes, prepare the couscous. Place the couscous in a big bowl, season and add the boiling water. The water should just cover the couscous. Cover the bowl with a plate and leave to stand for 10 minutes while you get on with the chops.

6 Trim any excess fat from the chops, rub them with olive oil and season. Heat a large frying pan over a medium-high heat and add the chops. Cook for 3–4 minutes on each side for medium rare (longer if you prefer well done). Place the cooked chops on a sheet of tin foil and wrap it to form a loose but firmly sealed parcel. Leave to rest for 3–4 minutes.

7 When they're fully cooked, remove the vegetables from the oven. Carefully take the garlic cloves out of the tray and squeeze the garlic pulp out of their skins into a small bowl. Mash the garlic with the back of a spoon, add the lemon juice and zest, mint and 1 teaspoon of olive oil and stir to make the dressing.

8 Uncover the couscous, fluff it up with a fork and stir in the vegetables, almonds (if using) and garlic dressing. Mix well.

9 To serve, divide the chops among warmed plates and drizzle them generously with the mint sauce. Serve with a nice helping of the vegetable couscous and tuck in!

WARM CHOCOLATE FUDGE SUNDAE WITH HONEYCOMB

I am without doubt an ice cream girl – and a purist, vanilla ice cream girl at that – so it's no wonder that I turn to ice cream desserts for a sweet fix. Fudge sundaes are the ultimate ice cream dessert. The silky smooth sauce in this one is dangerously addictive and will keep in a jar in the fridge for a few weeks. All you have to do is reheat it gently before serving – ideal if you want to prepare a dessert for people ahead of time.

I'm not expecting anyone to make honeycomb from scratch for this dessert: I simply chop up Crunchie bars, which gives the perfect effect. **Serves 4**

150 ml double cream
60 g milk chocolate, chopped into 1 cm pieces
60 g dark chocolate, chopped into 1 cm pieces
1 tablespoon golden syrup
15 g unsalted butter
good vanilla ice cream
2 Crunchie bars, roughly chopped
2 tablespoons salted peanuts, roughly chopped

1 Heat the cream in a medium pan over a medium heat. When it is just about to come to simmering point, add the chocolate, golden syrup and butter. Stir until everything is melted and the sauce is smooth and glossy. Remove from the heat.

2 Take some tall dessert glasses (or bowls if you don't have any) and put two big scoops of vanilla ice cream into each one. Scatter over the Crunchie pieces, drizzle over the warm fudge sauce and top with the peanuts. Irresistible!

SWEET AND SPICY STIR-FRY CHICKEN WITH FLUFFY RICE

Stir-fries are brilliant: you just bang a few ingredients in a wok or frying pan and, before you know it, dinner's ready. It's really important not to overload the pan when cooking stir-fries. The whole point of them is that everything is cooked quickly at a very high temperature. If your pan is too full, the heat won't reach all of the ingredients and they end up being slowly boiled instead of being nicely seared. So, stir-fry your ingredients in batches if needs be.

The fluffy rice method is one I learned in Ballymaloe and I've used it ever since. It's great because you don't need to worry about precision timing. You can prepare the rice in advance and leave it in the oven until you're ready to eat. It's especially good when you've people over for dinner and you want to make a large quantity without stressing.

This stir-fry is a homemade version of Chinese sweet and sour chicken – and it's so much nicer than anything you'd get in a takeaway! **Serves 4**

450 g basmati rice

olive oil

salt and freshly ground black pepper

4 chicken breasts, cut into thin strips

1 red pepper, finely sliced

1 yellow pepper, finely sliced

2 small red onions, finely sliced

3 red chillies, deseeded and finely chopped (use less if you don't want much heat)

3 garlic cloves, crushed

a thumb-sized piece of ginger, peeled and finely chopped

8 tablespoons soy sauce

6 tablespoons white wine

6 tablespoons tomato ketchup

4 tablespoons sugar

1 To make the rice, preheat the oven to 140°C/275°F/gas 1. Put the rice in a jug of cold water, stir, then drain. Repeat this in a few changes of water, then drain the rice in a sieve. Bring a large pan of water to a fast rolling boil and add a good pinch of salt. Add the drained rice, stir once, then boil rapidly without a lid for 4–5 minutes. Drain well and place the drained rice in an ovenproof dish. Cover the dish with tin foil and place in the oven until you're ready to eat. The rice will keep in the oven for up to 1 hour.

2 For the stir-fry, heat a few lugs of olive oil in a wok or large frying pan over a high heat. Season the chicken and add to the pan. Cook for about 5 minutes, until nicely browned, then remove to a bowl. Pour another lug of olive oil into the pan. When it's hot, add the peppers, onion, chillies, garlic and ginger. Stir-fry for 2–3 minutes. Meanwhile, mix the soy sauce, white wine, ketchup and sugar in a small bowl. Add to the vegetables in the pan, then return the chicken also. Stir-fry everything together for another 2 minutes.

3 Serve piping hot with the fluffy rice.

HEALTHY FRUIT AND OAT SNACK BARS

Most of us know what the afternoon slump is like: tiredness sets in and we automatically turn to coffee and a sugary snack for a pick-me-up. Of course, this energy never lasts: the sugars pick us up but bring us down just as quickly. Healthier snacks with natural sugars are a smart alternative and they'll keep you on the ball all day long!

These bars take a bit of forward planning but they really help during a busy week. The sweetness comes from the dried fruit, which gives you lots of nutrition. They're chewy and quite dense, so they'll definitely keep you going right through the afternoon. Adapt the recipe to use whatever nuts, fruits and seeds you prefer. There are endless variations to try, so you'll never be bored! The bars last in an airtight container for about a week. **Makes about 12 bars**

150 g porridge oats
40 g natural (unblanched) almonds, chopped
40 g pecan nuts, chopped
60 g sultanas
60 g dried apricots, chopped
60 g dried figs, chopped
15 g sunflower seeds
15 g sesame seeds
1 teaspoon cinnamon
salt
240 ml milk
1 egg
1 teaspoon vanilla extract

1 Preheat the oven to 180°C/350°F/gas 4. Grease a 20 cm (8 inch) square tin and line it with parchment paper.

2 Mix the oats, nuts, dried fruits and seeds in a large bowl. Stir in the cinnamon and a pinch of salt. Mix the milk, egg and vanilla extract in a small bowl. Pour the milk mixture into the oat mixture and stir well to combine. Pour into the lined tin and bake for 35–40 minutes, until golden.

3 Allow to cool in the tin before lifting out the baking parchment and cutting into squares.

THAI GREEN CURRY

Thai curries are delicious and I especially like ones that are packed with vegetables. Shop-bought Thai curry pastes are perfectly good to use and they make Thai curries really straightforward to cook. This green curry is a really tasty one and also very nutritious. If you prefer other vegetables, don't be afraid to experiment with different combinations. **Serves 4**

½ butternut squash, unpeeled, deseeded and cut into 2 cm pieces
1 red pepper, cut into 2 cm pieces
1 aubergine, cut into 2 cm pieces
salt and freshly ground black pepper
olive oil
½ onion, finely chopped
1 garlic clove, crushed
1 green chilli, deseeded and finely chopped
a thumb-sized piece of ginger, peeled and finely chopped
1 tablespoon Thai green curry paste
1 x 400 ml can coconut milk
200 ml vegetable stock, simmering
100 g frozen peas
75 g mangetout
juice of 1 lime
a handful of fresh coriander leaves (optional)

1 Preheat the oven to 200°C/400°F/gas 6.

2 Place the butternut squash, pepper and aubergine on a roasting tray. Add a lug of olive oil, season and mix well to coat evenly. Roast for 30 minutes, until the vegetables are completely soft, and set aside.

3 Heat a few lugs of olive oil in a large pan over a medium heat. Add the onion, garlic, chilli and ginger and cook for 2 minutes. Add the curry paste and cook for another minute. Add the coconut milk and stock, stir, and bring to the boil. Add the peas and mangetout and cook for 2 minutes, then add all the roasted vegetables. Stir well and allow to cook for a few minutes. Add lime juice and seasoning to taste.

4 Serve the curry on warmed plates with rice (see Fluffy Rice on p.58) and garnish with coriander leaves.

RHUBARB FOOL WITH ALMOND BISCUITS

Rhubarb... I think it's quite like Marmite: you either love it or hate it! I happen to love it and I buy lots of it for making desserts and jams when it comes into season in spring. Rhubarb fool is a favourite; the combination of the poached fruit with whipped cream is simply gorgeous and the bonus is that it's so easy to make. I've teamed the fool with some almond biscuits for a bit of crunch but it's perfectly good just on its own. Serves 6

450 g rhubarb, roughly chopped
150 g sugar
3 tablespoons water
280 ml double cream

For the almond biscuits
85 g butter
85 g caster sugar
55 g plain flour
85 g flaked almonds

1 Preheat the oven to 200°C/400°F/gas 6. Line two large baking sheets with parchment paper.

2 To make the biscuits, cream the butter and sugar in a large bowl with an electric beater, until pale and fluffy. Sift in the flour and stir. Add the flaked almonds and stir again. Drop heaped teaspoons of the mixture onto the lined baking sheets and flatten each biscuit with your fingers. Bake for 6–8 minutes, until golden, then remove from the oven. Leave the biscuits to cool on the trays for 1 minute before transferring to a wire rack.

3 To make the fool, place the rhubarb, sugar and water in a saucepan and simmer over a gentle heat for about 15 minutes, until completely soft. Stir with a wooden spoon to barely crush the rhubarb. Set aside and allow to cool completely.

4 Whip the cream until it forms soft peaks. (Don't over-whip the cream or it could separate when added to the rhubarb.) Drain the rhubarb, reserving the juice. Fold the rhubarb very gently into the cream, keeping the mixture quite textured and chunky.

5 Serve the fool in tall dessert glasses, with a few spoonfuls of the rhubarb juices drizzled over and some almond biscuits on the side.

SUMMER IS HERE! IT'S FUNNY HOW EVEN A LITTLE SUNSHINE HAS A WAY OF MAKING PEOPLE BEAM. FOR ME, MAY MEANS LONG WALKS IN THE EVENINGS, EATING OUTSIDE IN THE GARDEN (WHENEVER POSSIBLE) AND LOTS OF HEALTHY, FRESH SALADS TO USE UP ALL THE LOVELY SUMMER VEG THAT'S AVAILABLE.

MAY

SIRLOIN STEAK SALAD WITH ASIAN GREENS

When it's coming into summer, I start to crave salads packed with lots of fresh ingredients to make them nice and filling. Asian flavours work really well in salads, making them very refreshing. The dressing used in this salad is so tasty – it's one that works really well in lots of other salads, too. Serves 4

For the dressing
2 red chillies, deseeded and finely chopped
2 garlic cloves, crushed
3 tablespoons soy sauce
juice of 1 lime
4 tablespoons olive oil
2 teaspoons sugar

a handful of raw peanuts (optional)
4 x 150 g sirloin steaks, removed from the
    fridge 15 minutes before cooking
salt and freshly ground black pepper
olive oil
1 bunch of asparagus (about 12 spears)
1 head of broccoli, broken into small florets
100 g French beans, tails removed
4 handfuls of mixed baby salad leaves
a handful of fresh coriander leaves,
    roughly torn
a handful of fresh mint leaves, roughly torn

1 First prepare the dressing. Mix the chillies and garlic in a small bowl. Add the soy sauce, lime juice, olive oil and sugar. Mix well, taste, tweak the flavours to your liking and set aside.

2 Now roast the peanuts, if using. Heat a frying pan over a medium heat and add the peanuts to the dry pan. Stir them for about 5 minutes, until they're roasted. They will start to turn brown and the red skins will turn crisp and start to come away from the nuts. Empty the nuts into a clean tea towel, wrap it around them and rub the towel with your hands to remove the skins from the nuts. When most of the skins are gone, roughly chop the nuts and set aside.

3 Now cook the steaks. Heat a grill pan or frying pan over a high heat. Lay the steaks on a chopping board and trim off any excess fat. Sprinkle pepper on both sides of each steak, rub lightly with olive oil and, just before placing in the pan, sprinkle both sides with salt. Cook for 2–3 minutes each side for rare (see p.15 for other cooking times). Allow to rest on a plate for 5–10 minutes, then slice the steaks thinly.

4 Meanwhile, prepare the vegetables. Bend each asparagus stalk until it snaps. Each stalk will break in a different place, giving you different lengths of spears. Keep the spears and discard the woody ends. Add the asparagus spears, broccoli and French beans to a large pan of boiling salted water, ensuring they are completely submerged. Boil rapidly for 4–5 minutes, until the vegetables are just cooked and retain a little bite. Drain in a colander.

5 Arrange the salad leaves and herbs in a large serving dish. Just before serving, add the cooked vegetables, drizzle over the dressing and toss well. Scatter the steak slices on top and sprinkle with the peanuts. Serve immediately.

MUM'S EPIC CHOCOLATE MOUSSE

My mum was a huge influence in my early cooking years. Watching her in the kitchen inspired me and without that experience I'm sure I wouldn't be half the cook I am today. This chocolate mousse is the dessert my mother is known for amongst her friends. I remember many occasions when I carried a big glass bowl of it with me, as my brother and I were dragged to someone's house for dinner! Nowadays, I often make it for my friends and it truly is the best chocolate mousse I've ever had. **Serves 8**

335 g dark chocolate (60% cocoa solids), roughly chopped
8 eggs, separated

1 Place the chocolate in a heatproof bowl over a saucepan of simmering water. Make sure the bottom of the bowl doesn't touch the water. Don't stir until the chocolate is almost melted, then give it a gentle stir to help it along. Once the chocolate has melted, scrape it into a large mixing bowl and allow to cool.

2 Place the egg yolks in a medium bowl and beat lightly with a wooden spoon. Place the egg whites in a clean, dry bowl and whisk with an electric beater until they form soft peaks.

3 When the chocolate has cooled completely, gradually mix in the egg yolks. Then, very gently, gradually fold in the egg whites in batches.

4 Pour the mousse into a glass serving bowl and leave in the fridge to set for a few hours – overnight would be even better.

ROAST ASPARAGUS IN PARMA HAM

Asparagus, when it's just come into season, is absolutely to die for. I eat lots of it in the summer, when it's plentiful, as it makes a lovely light lunch or healthy starter. This dish involves the classic combination of asparagus and Parma ham. It can also be easily transformed into an impressive starter for a dinner party if you serve it with some homemade hollandaise sauce. **Serves 4**

2 bunches of asparagus (24 spears)
2 tablespoons olive oil
2 tablespoons balsamic vinegar, plus extra for drizzling
salt and freshly ground black pepper
8 slices Parma ham

1 Preheat the oven to 180°C/350°F/gas 4.

2 Bend each asparagus stalk until it snaps. Each stalk will break in a different place, giving you different lengths of spears. Keep the spears and discard the woody ends. Cook the asparagus in a pan of boiling salted water for 2 minutes, then drain and refresh under cold running water.

3 Place the asparagus in a large bowl and drizzle over the olive oil and balsamic vinegar. Season and toss well. Wrap a slice of Parma ham around 3 asparagus spears. Continue with the remaining ham and asparagus, until you have 8 snug bundles. Arrange the bundles in an ovenproof dish and roast for 10 minutes, until the ham is nice and crisp.

4 To serve, divide the bundles among warmed serving plates and drizzle with balsamic vinegar.

LEMON CRUNCH

*I love this simple, summery dessert. It's a creamy, crunchy, lemony dream... **Serves 4–6***

55 g butter
170 g Digestive biscuits
140 g Demerara or brown sugar, divided
1 egg, plus 2 eggs separated
zest of 2 lemons, juice of 1 lemon
pinch of salt
285 ml double cream

1 Melt the butter in a small pan over a low heat. While the butter is melting, bash the Digestive biscuits into crumbs. You can put them in a Ziploc bag and bash them with a rolling pin or just break them with your hands. Place the Digestive crumbs in a bowl and mix in 25 g of the sugar. Stir in the melted butter and set aside.

2 Whisk the whole egg, plus 2 egg yolks, in a bowl with an electric beater. Add the remaining sugar (115 g), lemon zest and juice, and a pinch of salt. Beat well.

3 Place the 2 egg whites in a large, clean, dry bowl and whisk with an electric beater until they form stiff peaks. In a separate bowl, whip the cream until it holds soft peaks. Fold the cream into the egg yolk mixture, then fold this mixture into the large bowl with the whisked egg whites.

4 Sprinkle a layer of the crumbs on the bottom of a large glass serving bowl. Spoon a layer of the lemon mixture evenly on top. Add another layer of crumbs and repeat this layering, finishing with a crumb layer on top. Chill well in the fridge before serving. Delish!

CHICKEN AND BROCCOLI GRATIN

This is a brilliant recipe for using up leftover chicken from a Sunday roast, but I like it so much that I've often made it from scratch with chicken breasts. A lot of gratins have cream in the recipe but I've used milk here, which makes it a healthier dish. It's a whole meal in itself and it's delicious served with a green side salad. Serves 4

olive oil
600 g cooked chicken, diced, or 4 chicken breasts, diced
salt and freshly ground black pepper
1 large head of broccoli, broken into florets
50 g butter, divided
25 g plain flour
500 ml milk
200 ml chicken stock, simmering
1 onion, finely chopped
100 g breadcrumbs
2 tablespoons chopped fresh parsley
1 tablespoon chopped fresh rosemary

1 Preheat the oven to 180°C/350°F/gas 4. If using chicken breasts, heat a few lugs of olive oil in a frying pan over a medium-high heat. Season the chicken pieces and fry for about 5 minutes until cooked and golden brown. Set aside.

2 Cook the broccoli in a large pan of boiling salted water for 2–3 minutes. Drain in a colander and refresh under cold running water. Place the broccoli on a clean tea towel and set aside to dry.

3 Melt half the butter (25 g) in a medium pan over a medium heat. Add the flour and cook for 1 minute, stirring briskly. Add the milk a little at a time, and bring it up to simmering point, whisking continuously with a balloon whisk. Add the stock and season. Return to a simmer and cook the sauce for a few minutes more, whisking all the time to make a thick, pouring consistency. Stir the chicken and broccoli into the sauce and mix well. Pour the mixture into an ovenproof dish and set aside.

4 Melt the remaining butter (25 g) in a medium saucepan and fry the onion for 3–4 minutes, until softened. Stir in the breadcrumbs and chopped herbs and season. Spread the breadcrumbs evenly over the chicken and broccoli mixture and bake for 20 minutes until the breadcrumbs are golden brown.

5 Bring the gratin straight to the table and let everyone tuck in.

FISH GOUJONS WITH QUICK TARTARE SAUCE AND MINTY PEA PURÉE

This dish is like posh fish fingers and peas! Homemade fish goujons made with really fresh fish are melt-in-your-mouth delicious. I adore tartare sauce with white fish and this tartare recipe is great for whipping together in just a few minutes. The minted pea purée is lovely and doesn't take much effort. Serve this dish with chips or the Roast Baby Potatoes on p.15. **Serves 4**

For the tartare sauce
100 g mayonnaise
1 teaspoon capers, finely chopped
2 $\frac{1}{2}$ teaspoons gherkins, finely chopped
1 tablespoon finely chopped fresh parsley
grated zest of $\frac{1}{2}$ lemon, plus lemon juice to taste
salt and freshly ground black pepper

300 g frozen peas
a handful of fresh mint
milk (optional)
160 g breadcrumbs
2 teaspoons paprika
5 heaped tablespoons plain flour
2 eggs
4 x 180 g white fish fillets, skinned, pinboned and cut into thin strips (cod, plaice and haddock work well)
sunflower oil, for shallow-frying

1 To make the tartare sauce, mix the mayonnaise, capers, gherkins, parsley and lemon zest in a small bowl. Add lemon juice to taste, and set aside.

2 Cook the peas in a pan of boiling salted water for 2–3 minutes. Drain and place in a food processor with the mint. Blitz to form a rough paste, season and add some milk if you want a thinner consistency. Keep the purée warm while you prepare the fish.

3 Mix the breadcrumbs, paprika and some seasoning in a wide dish. Place the flour on a plate. Lightly beat the eggs in a bowl. Roll each fish strip in the flour, shaking off any excess. Dip each fish strip into the beaten egg, then roll each one in the breadcrumbs until completely coated.

4 Fill a wide, high-sided frying pan with sunflower oil to about an inch high and place on a medium-high heat, until a breadcrumb sizzles and turns golden when dropped in. Fry the fish goujons in batches for 2–3 minutes until cooked through and golden brown. Remove with a slotted spoon and drain on kitchen paper on a warm plate.

5 Divide the goujons and pea purée among warmed plates and serve with some tartare sauce and lemon wedges.

MELKTERT

My mum grew up in South Africa and this traditional South African pudding is one that she made a lot when I was a kid. I vividly remember how chuffed she was when she won the bake-off in our local village with her Melktert ('milk tart' in Afrikaans). None of the other ladies or the judges had ever tried a tart like it before, which I think clinched it for her.

I find the filling in this tart really moreish and, as they say in South Africa, 'very lekker' (yummy)! This dessert summons such nostalgia for me that I couldn't write a cookbook without it featuring. I hope you enjoy it as much as I do. **Makes one 30 cm tart (or two 15 cm tarts)**

500 g ready-made shortcrust pastry, thawed if frozen
30 g butter
830 ml milk
2 ½ tablespoons flour, plus extra for dusting
2 ½ tablespoons cornflour
3 eggs
170 g caster sugar
a few drops of vanilla extract
cinnamon

1 Preheat the oven to 180°C/350°F/gas 4.

2 Roll out the pastry to 5 mm thickness on a lightly floured board and use it to line a buttered 30 cm (12 inch) tart tin with removable base. Prick the pastry with a fork. Line the pastry case with greaseproof paper and fill to the top with baking beans or dried pulses. Bake for 15 minutes, then remove from the oven. Carefully remove the beans and greaseproof paper. Brush the pastry case with some beaten egg and return it to the oven to bake for a further 5 minutes, until golden.

3 Meanwhile, put the butter and most of the milk (keeping back a few tablespoons) into a medium saucepan over a low heat and gently bring to the boil.

4 Place the remaining few tablespoons of milk in a bowl, add the flour and cornflour and stir to make a paste. Beat the eggs and sugar into the paste and mix well.

5 Be careful not to let the milk in the pan boil over. Just as it comes to the boil, tip in the bowl of paste. Quickly reduce the heat and whisk continuously with a balloon whisk, until it thickens. Be patient and allow it to thicken to the consistency of custard, whisking all the time to make sure no lumps form. Remove from the heat, stir in the vanilla extract and pour this filling into the pastry base. Sieve a little cinnamon powder over the tart and leave to cool. Once it has cooled a bit, transfer the tart to the fridge and leave it to set for 1–2 hours before serving.

LEMON AND GARLIC LAMB CHOPS WITH PEANUT PESTO AND CHILLI POTATO SALAD

In summertime I use lemons in cooking as often as I use salt and pepper! I can't resist the zesty freshness that lemon adds to food, especially when the weather is warm. This dish uses lots of lemon, which works really well with the lamb. The potato salad is a fresh and light variation on classic potato salad. The pesto recipe came about one day when I didn't have any pine nuts to hand so I substituted peanuts and was delighted with the result. **Serves 4**

For the lamb

2 garlic cloves, crushed

2 tablespoons olive oil

juice of I lemon

8 lamb loin chops

For the potato salad

I kg potatoes, peeled

3 tablespoons olive oil

juice of ¹/₂ lemon

salt and freshly ground black pepper

I large green chilli, deseeded and finely chopped

a handful of chopped fresh mint

a handful of chopped fresh parsley

For the pesto

a few handfuls of basil leaves, about 100 g

70 g salted peanuts

2–3 garlic cloves

juice of I lemon

80–100 ml olive oil

1 For the lamb, mix the garlic, olive oil and lemon juice in a large bowl. Add the lamb and mix well. Cover and leave to marinate in the fridge for 20–30 minutes while you prepare the pesto and salad.

2 Cook the potatoes in a large pan of boiling salted water for 15–20 minutes until just tender. Drain well. When cool enough to handle, cut the potatoes into quarters. Mix the olive oil and lemon juice in a large bowl, add the potatoes, season and mix gently. Add the chilli, mint and parsley and mix gently until combined.

3 Put all the pesto ingredients except the olive oil in a food processor. Blitz and gradually add the olive oil until the pesto is well blended and it reaches your desired consistency. Taste, tweak the flavours to your liking and set aside.

4 Heat a large frying pan over a medium-high heat. Remove the lamb chops from the marinade, season and fry for 3–4 minutes on each side for medium rare (longer if you prefer well done). Place the cooked chops on a sheet of tin foil and wrap it to form a loose but firmly sealed parcel. Leave to rest for 3–4 minutes.

5 Place two chops on each warmed serving plate, spoon some pesto on the chops and serve with a generous helping of potato salad on the side.

JUNE

JUNE SCREAMS STRAWBERRIES AND CREAM – SYNONYMOUS WITH WIMBLEDON, OF COURSE. DURING THE SCHOOL HOLIDAYS, I PLAYED TENNIS EVERY DAY WITH MY MUM; AND WE STILL JOKE ABOUT HOW MANY YEARS IT TOOK HER TO PART WITH THAT OLD-FASHIONED, WOODEN RACKET OF HERS!

THESE DAYS I'M STILL GLUED TO THE TENNIS AT THE END OF JUNE. IT'S MY RITUAL TO PERCH MYSELF ON THE SOFA AND WATCH MATCH AFTER MATCH, WHILE INDULGING IN A SUMMERY STRAWBERRY DESSERT. SOME OF THE DESSERTS IN THIS CHAPTER CONTAIN STRAWBERRIES; AND EVERY RECIPE IN THIS CHAPTER IS AS EASY AS IT IS IRRESISTIBLE...

ROAST ASPARAGUS AND TOMATOES WITH BAKED POTATOES

My dad impressed me by cooking this vegetarian meal for dinner one evening – it's gorgeous and really healthy, too. The key to it is to use good tomatoes and asparagus when they're in season and at their tastiest. For me, the beauty of this dish is its simplicity: you just throw a few ingredients in the oven and then relax until they're ready. Perfect! **Serves 4**

2 bunches of asparagus (about 24 spears)
olive oil
500 g cherry tomatoes, halved
3 green chillies, deseeded and finely chopped
a handful of fresh basil leaves, roughly torn
salt and freshly ground black pepper
4 large potatoes, washed and unpeeled

1 Preheat the oven to 200°C/400°F/gas 6.

2 Bend each asparagus stalk until it snaps. Each stalk will break in a different place, giving you different lengths of spears. Keep the spears and discard the woody ends. Pour a few lugs of olive oil into a large ovenproof dish. Place the asparagus, tomatoes, chillies and basil in the dish, season and mix well to coat evenly. Set aside.

3 Wrap each potato in tin foil and bake for 1 hour. For the final 12 minutes of cooking, place the vegetables in the oven also.

4 When the potatoes and vegetables are cooked, cut the potatoes in half and mash them up a bit with a fork. Pour the vegetables and all their lovely juices over the potatoes. Drizzle a little extra olive oil on top, if you fancy, and tuck in!

CARAMEL, PEACH AND ALMOND CAKE

This is a gorgeous upside-down cake in which the peaches are placed in caramel and then the almond sponge mix is poured on top before being baked in the oven. When you turn the cake over, you have the most stunning-looking dessert.

It's such a simple cake to make and it's a complete winner if you're having friends over: it looks so impressive that they'll think you're amazing! The combination of the peaches and the almond sponge is super. **Serves 8–10**

240 g caster sugar
150 ml water
400 g peaches (about 6 peaches), stoned and quartered

For the almond sponge
170 g caster sugar
150 g butter, at room temperature
3 eggs
120 g self-raising flour
80 g ground almonds

1 Preheat the oven to 180°C/350°F/gas 4.

2 Place the 240 g caster sugar and the water in an ovenproof frying pan with a diameter of about 25 cm (10 inches). Turn the heat to medium and stir until the sugar dissolves completely. Once the sugar dissolves, stop stirring and leave the sugar to caramelise and turn a golden brown colour. Be patient: it can take a little while before it starts to caramelise, but once you see it turning brown around the edges, it will happen very quickly. At this point, tilt the pan from side to side to encourage the caramel to spread. Do not let the caramel get too dark or it will have a burnt taste. As soon as the caramel takes a golden brown colour, remove the pan from the heat.

3 Carefully arrange the peach quarters on top of the caramel in the pan. I like to arrange them in a circular pattern starting from the outside and working all the way into the centre of the pan, so it looks like a big swirl. Try to cover all the caramel with peach pieces.

4 Place all the almond sponge ingredients in a food processor and blitz until just combined. Don't over-mix. Gently pour the sponge mix over the peaches and smooth into an even layer using a spatula.

5 Place the pan in the oven and bake for 50–60 minutes, or until the centre is firm and the edges of the cake are starting to come away from the pan. Leave to cool for 5–10 minutes. To invert the cake, you'll need a plate wider than the cake pan. Place the plate (serving side facing down) on top of the cake pan and quickly flip them over. Take the cake pan away to reveal the most gorgeous caramel peach cake!

6 Serve warm or cold with cream or crème fraîche.

STRAWBERRY SHORTBREAD STACKS

Who doesn't love strawberries and cream in summertime? Of course they taste great served on their own, but team them with light, flaky, buttery shortbread biscuits and they make a gorgeous little summer dessert. I use mascarpone cream in this recipe, which tastes amazing with the shortbread. **Serves 4**

For the shortbread
100 g butter, at room temperature
100 g plain flour, plus extra for dusting
55 g icing sugar
1 egg yolk

For the filling
200 g strawberries, hulled and sliced horizontally (if your slices are straight, stacking will be easier)
1 teaspoon finely grated lemon zest
200 g mascarpone
1 tablespoon double cream
1 teaspoon vanilla extract
1 tablespoon icing sugar, plus extra for dusting

1 Preheat the oven to 180°C/350°F/gas 4. Line two large baking sheets with parchment paper.

2 Place the butter, flour, icing sugar and egg yolk in a food processor and blitz until it just comes together to form a dough. Roll the dough to 5 mm thickness on a lightly floured board and cut into rounds with a 6 cm cutter. (If you don't have a cutter, use a knife to cut 6 cm squares.) Re-roll the excess dough and repeat until the dough is used up. Place the dough shapes on the lined baking trays, leaving space between them. Bake for 8–10 minutes, until pale golden. Remove the trays from the oven and allow the biscuits to cool on the tray.

3 Place the strawberries and lemon zest in a small bowl. Stir carefully and set aside. In a separate bowl, mix the mascarpone, cream, vanilla extract and icing sugar until combined.

4 Once the shortbread biscuits have cooled, you can assemble the stacks. Place half the biscuits on a board. (Leave aside the other half for now – they'll be used to top the stacks.) Place a layer of strawberry slices on each shortbread base. Now spoon a layer of mascarpone mixture on top of each strawberry layer, dividing evenly until all the mascarpone mixture is used. Add a second layer of strawberry slices. Finally, top each stack with a shortbread biscuit and dust with icing sugar. Garnish with any leftover strawberries and serve.

Peanut sauce is popular in many different Asian cuisines and it's one of those sauces you can really experiment with. You can keep it mild or you can use lots of chilli to spice it up. You can change the texture by using chopped roasted peanuts or peanut butter. You can make it thick and creamy with coconut milk or keep it light with water. Anything goes!

It's so quick to put together that it's great for a midweek meal. This is my favourite version and it makes a large amount, so halve it if you want. I like to make a big batch, though, since the leftovers keep in the fridge for weeks. Serves 4

3 tablespoons peanut butter
3 tablespoons sweet chilli sauce
2 tablespoons soy sauce
juice of 1 lime
4 nests of medium egg noodles
olive oil
4 chicken breasts, cut into thin strips

a thumb-sized piece of fresh ginger, peeled and grated
1 green pepper, finely sliced
1 red pepper, finely sliced
a handful of mangetout
salt and freshly ground black pepper
a handful of basil leaves, roughly torn
1 scallion, finely sliced (optional)

1 Mix the peanut butter, chilli sauce, soy sauce, lime juice and 100 ml water in a pan over a medium heat. Don't worry if it looks like it's not mixing together; as soon as it heats up, it will come together nicely. Slowly bring to the boil, stirring all the time, until it thickens and turns into a smooth peanut sauce. Remove from the heat and set aside.

2 Place the noodle nests in a large heatproof bowl and pour boiling water over them. Use a fork to separate the noodles, leave them for a minute, then drain thoroughly.

3 Heat a few lugs of olive oil in a wok or large frying pan over a high heat. Add the chicken strips, season and stir-fry for about 5 minutes, until golden. Once the chicken is just cooked, remove from the pan and set aside.

4 Heat a little more olive oil in the pan, add the ginger, peppers and mangetout and stir-fry for about 2 minutes. (When stir-frying vegetables, it can help to add a splash of water to the pan. This creates steam, which helps vegetables cook quicker.) Add the drained noodles and stir-fry for another minute or two, adding a splash of water if the noodles stick.

5 Return the chicken to the pan and pour in enough of the peanut sauce to lightly coat everything. Mix well and heat through. Divide the stir-fry onto warmed plates and sprinkle over the basil leaves and scallion. Serve immediately.

ROAST STUFFED MUSHROOMS WITH CHERRY TOMATOES

Roasting large mushrooms with fillings is a great idea for a starter. They are really easy to prepare and look very impressive for the amount of effort involved – not to mention how delicious they taste. I particularly like the filling in this recipe but there are endless options, so experiment! Serves 4

50 g raw cashew nuts
150 g mozzarella, torn
15 ml cream
20 g breadcrumbs
grated zest and juice of ½ lemon
pinch of cayenne pepper or chilli powder
4 large Portobello mushrooms, cleaned and stems removed
400 g cherry tomatoes, whole (on or off the vine)
olive oil
salt and freshly ground black pepper

1 Preheat the oven to 200°C/400°F/gas 6.

2 Heat a small pan over a medium heat and add the cashews. Toast them for a few minutes, tossing regularly, until golden. Remove the cashews from the pan, leave them to cool, then roughly chop them.

3 Mix the mozzarella, cream, breadcrumbs, lemon zest and juice, cayenne pepper and chopped cashews in a bowl and season well. Spoon this mixture into the hollow part of the mushrooms and place them in an ovenproof dish. Drizzle with a little olive oil and roast for 20 minutes or until golden brown.

4 Meanwhile, heat a few lugs of olive oil in a frying pan over a medium-high heat. Add the cherry tomatoes and sauté for about 15 minutes, until the skins split open and soften.

5 When the mushrooms are cooked, place them on warmed serving plates and top with the cherry tomatoes. Season to taste and serve.

PLAICE PARCELS WITH PARSLEY BUTTER, AND AVOCADO AND TOMATO SALAD

Fish makes a lovely, light dinner during the summer months. This dish can be made with other fresh white fish, such as sole, and baking in the paper parcels keeps the fish lovely and soft. I love the combination of avocado and tomatoes in this salad; it goes really nicely with the fish. If you want to bulk it up, serve some crusty bread or potatoes on the side. ***Serves 4***

50 g butter, at room temperature
1 tablespoon chopped fresh parsley
4 x 180 g plaice fillets, skinned and pinboned
salt and freshly ground black pepper
2 avocados
400 g cherry tomatoes, halved
a handful of basil leaves, torn
balsamic vinegar
olive oil

1 Preheat the oven to 200°C/400°F/gas 6.

2 Beat the butter and parsley in a small bowl, until smooth. Cut out four large sheets of parchment paper and place a fish fillet in the centre of each sheet. Season, and dot each fillet with a spoonful of parsley butter (use up all the butter if you wish). Wrap each sheet to form a loose but firmly sealed parcel. Bake for about 10 minutes, until the fish is just done and has turned opaque.

3 Meanwhile, cut each avocado. Run a knife all the way around the avocado, from top to bottom. Make sure you cut in until the blade meets the stone. Twist the two halves in opposite directions to separate them. Ease the stone out with a spoon. Cut the flesh of the avocado in a cross-hatch pattern, being careful not to break the skin. Pop the avocado halves inside out and the avocado squares should come away easily with a spoon. Place them in a big bowl with the tomatoes and basil. Drizzle with a few lugs of balsamic vinegar and a lug of olive oil. Season and mix well.

4 Serve each fish parcel on a warmed plate, allowing your guests to unwrap the parcels themselves so that all the lovely, buttery juices run onto their plates. Serve a generous helping of the avocado and tomato salad on the side.

ROAST SALMON SALAD WITH BROAD BEANS, PEPPERS AND AVOCADO

This is a super-healthy and tasty salad. It makes the most out of broad beans, which are among my favourite summer vegetables. They're at their best and easily available in June; and they're so deliciously sweet that I can't let the month go by without having some! The combination of the vegetables and salmon in this recipe is really yummy – and even more enjoyable when you think how healthy it is. **Serves 4**

For the dressing
4 tablespoons olive oil
2 tablespoons white wine vinegar
I teaspoon Dijon mustard
2 teaspoons sugar
I garlic clove, crushed
salt and freshly ground black pepper

2 red peppers, whole
olive oil
4 x 170 g skinless salmon fillets
100 g broad beans, shelled
2 avocados
4 handfuls of mixed baby salad leaves
a handful of basil leaves, torn

1 Preheat the oven to 200°C/400°F/gas 6.

2 Use a balloon whisk to mix all the dressing ingredients in a small bowl. Season and set aside.

3 Rub the peppers lightly with olive oil. Place them in an ovenproof dish and roast for 30 minutes.

4 Season the salmon fillets, rub lightly with oil and place in another ovenproof dish. When the peppers are 30 minutes in the oven, place the salmon in the oven, too. Roast everything for a further 10 minutes, until the peppers are blackened and the salmon is just cooked.

5 Remove the salmon fillets to a plate to cool. Once cooled, flake the salmon into chunks.

6 Meanwhile, put the cooked peppers in a bowl covered with cling film and leave to cool. The steam in the bowl will make the peppers easier to peel. After 15 minutes, carefully peel the peppers using your fingers. Ensure that you do not rinse the peppers or discard any of the lovely juices that have formed at the bottom of the bowl. Remove the stalks, cores and seeds from the peppers and cut into thin slices.

7 Cook the broad beans in a pan of boiling salted water for 2–3 minutes, until tender. Drain and refresh under cold running water until cool.

8 Now, dice each avocado. Run a knife all the way around the avocado, from top to bottom. Make sure you cut in until the blade meets the stone. Twist the two halves in opposite directions to separate them. Ease the stone out with a spoon. Cut the flesh of the avocado in a cross-hatch pattern, being careful not to break the skin. Pop the avocado halves inside out and the avocado squares should come away easily with a spoon.

9 Mix the salad leaves, salmon, avocados, pepper strips and their juices, and broad beans in a large bowl. Drizzle over the dressing, tossing until everything is coated, then scatter over the basil leaves.

10 Divide the salad among serving plates. This salad is very filling, but you could serve it with some boiled new potatoes or crusty bread.

MINI STRAWBERRY CHEESECAKES

This is a shortcut recipe for strawberry cheesecake and it makes for an impressive-looking dessert. It doesn't need to be baked and, because you prepare the cheesecakes in individual glasses, they set a lot quicker than one large cheesecake would. Ideal for a midweek dessert.
Serves 4

50 g butter (preferably unsalted)
100 g Digestive biscuits
500 g mascarpone
50 g icing sugar, sieved
1 teaspoon vanilla extract
400 g strawberries, hulled and quartered, divided

For the sauce
2 tablespoons lemon juice
1 tablespoon caster sugar

1 Melt the butter in a small pan over a low heat. While the butter is melting, bash the Digestive biscuits into crumbs. You can put them in a Ziploc bag and bash them with a rolling pin or just break them with your hands. Mix the melted butter and biscuit crumbs in a bowl, then divide the mixture among 4 serving glasses, pressing down well. Place the serving glasses in the fridge to chill for about 10 minutes.

2 Mix the mascarpone, icing sugar and vanilla extract in a large bowl, until well combined. Then stir in 300 g strawberries (leaving the remaining 100 g aside for now). It looks well if the strawberry juices start to ooze into the mascarpone. Set aside.

3 Now make the sauce. Place the remaining strawberries (100 g) in a food processor, along with the lemon juice and sugar. Blitz until smooth. Taste, and add more sugar if needed.

4 Remove the serving glasses from the fridge. Divide the mascarpone mixture evenly among the glasses. Finish with a generous drizzling of strawberry sauce.

5 You can chill the cheesecakes until you're ready to eat. If you can't wait, don't worry: they're delicious eaten straight away!

JULY

SCHOOL'S OUT! THE DISTANT MUSIC OF AN ICE CREAM VAN IS A FAMILIAR SOUND NEAR MY HOUSE. IT REMINDS ME OF SUMMER DAYS SPENT RUNNING AROUND THE PHOENIX PARK, PLAYING FRISBEE AND ROLLING DOWN HILLS, WEARING OURSELVES OUT UNTIL IT WAS TIME TO RELAX WITH A CREAMY 99.

AS AN ADULT, I STILL LOVE GOING TO THE PARK (WITHOUT THE ROLLING DOWN HILLS PART!) AND THE ODD TIME I EVEN INDULGE IN SOME NOSTALGIA BY QUEUING WITH THE KIDS FOR AN ENORMOUS, SUPER-SOFT WHIPPY. JULY DAYS ARE GREAT DAYS...

CLASSIC CARBONARA

Ordering spaghetti carbonara in a restaurant can be hit and miss. I've tried some very stodgy ones, which were far too heavy for me, but this recipe makes a lovely carbonara without using any cream. To make the carbonara sauce, you just need eggs, bacon and Parmesan; and if you don't have spaghetti, use another type of pasta. The simplicity of this dish makes it a perfect choice for busy weeknights. **Serves 4**

400 g spaghetti
salt and freshly ground black pepper
olive oil
1 garlic clove, peeled and left whole
8 slices pancetta or smoky bacon, diced
3 eggs, beaten
80 g finely grated Parmesan

1 Cook the spaghetti in a large pan of boiling salted water, according to packet instructions. Don't break the spaghetti: just stand it in the pan and, as the ends soften, slide the rest in. Always cook pasta in a large volume of water. The Italians say the water should be as salty as sea water, so use plenty of salt and you won't have to season after cooking. Cook the pasta until al dente (tender but firm to the bite).

2 Meanwhile, heat a lug of olive oil in a large pan over a medium-high heat. Place the garlic clove on a chopping board and crush it slightly with the flat of a large knife. Add the garlic and pancetta to the pan and fry until the pancetta is golden. Remove from the heat and discard the garlic clove now, as it has released its flavour.

3 Mix the eggs and Parmesan in a large bowl until combined, then season.

4 Drain the spaghetti, but keep back some of the cooking water and put it aside. Stir the spaghetti and a few tablespoons of the cooking water into the pan with the pancetta and mix well to combine.

5 Now tip all the contents of the pan into the egg and cheese mixture in the bowl. Use a tongs to lift the spaghetti several times so that it mixes well but doesn't scramble the eggs. Do this until all the spaghetti is coated. Add a few more tablespoons of the cooking water to keep the sauce glossy and moist. You don't want it too wet, so add just enough to give the sauce a nice coating consistency.

6 Serve immediately in warmed bowls with a good grinding of black pepper.

CHERRY CLAFOUTIS

Clafoutis is a traditional, rustic French dessert in which cherries are baked in a light, custard-like batter, and it is then served warm with a dusting of icing sugar. I think cherries have to be my favourite summer fruit – I could just munch on them all day long! July is a great month for cherries and clafoutis is a great way to use them because it's really easy to make.

If you can't find cherries, you could use another soft summer fruit. This dessert is best eaten when it's just made, so it's better not to cook it too far in advance. **Serves 4–6**

350–400 g cherries, stoned
80 g sugar, plus extra for sprinkling
3 eggs
1/2 teaspoon vanilla extract
salt
300 ml milk
80 g plain flour
icing sugar, to serve

1 Preheat the oven to 180°C/350°F/gas 4. Grease a 25 cm (10 inch) baking dish and sprinkle 2 tablespoons of sugar over the base of the dish. Dot the cherries around the base of the dish.

2 Whisk the sugar, eggs, vanilla extract and a pinch of salt in a large bowl with an electric beater, until smooth. Add the milk and whisk again. Sift the flour into the mixture and whisk until blended. Set this batter aside for ten minutes, then pour it over the cherries.

3 Bake for 30–35 minutes, until the clafoutis is golden and set, and a skewer inserted in the centre comes out clean. Serve warm with a dusting of icing sugar over the top.

BEST-EVER STEAK SANDWICH

A steak sandwich is one of those things that if it's not done properly, can be mediocre; but if it's done properly, it's outstanding! This recipe is my idea of the perfect combination necessary for the best steak sandwich ever. I don't like to complicate it by adding too many fillings because it really doesn't need it – keep it simple and enjoy. **Serves 4**

For the caramelised onions
olive oil
2 red onions, finely sliced
I teaspoon caster sugar
2 tablespoons balsamic vinegar

For the garlic mayonnaise
170 ml mayonnaise
I tablespoon balsamic vinegar
2 garlic cloves, crushed
salt and freshly ground black pepper

700 g sirloin or rump steak, cut into 4 x 2 cm steaks, removed from the fridge
   15 minutes before cooking
I large ciabatta loaf, halved lengthways and cut into four (to make 8 slices)
a few handfuls of rocket leaves

1 Heat a few lugs of olive oil in a large frying pan over a medium heat. Add the onions and fry for 10 minutes, until soft. Add the sugar and balsamic vinegar and cook for another 2 minutes, until reduced and caramelised. Remove the onions from the pan and set aside. (If you don't have a separate grill pan for cooking the steaks, keep this frying pan aside and reuse it later.)

2 For the garlic mayonnaise, combine the mayonnaise, balsamic vinegar and garlic in a small bowl. Mix well and season to taste.

3 Heat a grill pan over a high heat. Sprinkle pepper on both sides of each steak, rub lightly with olive oil and, just before placing in the pan, sprinkle both sides with salt. Cook for 2–3 minutes each side for rare (see p.15 for other cooking times). Transfer the steaks to a plate to rest.

4 Drizzle the ciabatta slices with olive oil. Arrange them on a grill rack and place under the grill until lightly toasted. Once the steaks have rested, cut them into thin strips.

5 Spread each ciabatta slice with plenty of garlic mayonnaise. Take 4 of the ciabatta slices (the bases) and pile on the caramelised onions, steak strips and some rocket leaves. Top with the remaining ciabatta slices and stand back as everyone devours the sandwiches!

MERINGUE NESTS WITH RASPBERRY CREAM FILLING

The great thing about meringues is their versatility: you can add so many different fillings and flavours to them. This recipe makes a gorgeous summertime dessert. You could use shop-bought meringues if you're in a hurry, but homemade ones are in a different league altogether. I've used a raspberry cream filling here, which is delicious, but feel free to experiment. **Serves 4**

For the meringues
3 egg whites, at room temperature
175 g caster sugar

For the raspberry coulis
240 g raspberries
2 tablespoons icing sugar
1 tablespoon lemon juice

200 ml double cream
2 tablespoons icing sugar, sieved

1 Preheat the oven to 130°C/250°F/gas mark ½. Line 2 large baking sheets with parchment paper.

2 Place the egg whites in a large, dry bowl and whisk on maximum speed with an electric whisk, until stiff. Add the sugar a tablespoon at a time and continue whisking, still at top speed, until the mixture is very stiff and all the sugar has been added. The mixture will take on a lovely, glossy appearance.

3 Scoop out heaped dessertspoonfuls of the meringue and drop them onto the baking trays, leaving plenty of space between them. Use the back of the spoon to make a little hollow in the centre of each meringue. Bake for 1 hour, until crisp. Turn off the oven and leave the meringues in there to cool.

4 Meanwhile, make the coulis. Place the raspberries, icing sugar and lemon juice in a food processor and blitz to a purée. Push the purée through a sieve over a bowl, to remove the raspberry seeds. Taste and add more sugar if needs be.

5 Lightly whip the cream and stir in the icing sugar. Then stir the raspberry coulis into the cream.

6 Once the meringues have cooled fully, spoon the raspberry cream mixture into the hollow of each meringue and serve.

CRISPY CARAMELISED CHICKEN THIGHS WITH LEMON AND CORIANDER RICE

This is a really easy and economical meal to cook and it definitely doesn't lack in taste! Chicken thighs are much better value than chicken breasts, and thigh meat actually has a lot more flavour. I love how the chicken skin caramelises and turns crispy from the marinade in this dish – it's so good. The lemon and coriander rice is a nice way to liven up plain rice and it goes particularly well with the chicken here. Serves 4

For the marinade
2 tablespoons natural yogurt
2 tablespoons sweet chilli sauce
3 garlic cloves, crushed
a thumb-sized piece of ginger, grated
1 tablespoon curry powder
8 chicken thighs (bone in, with skin)

For the rice
350 g basmati rice
grated zest and juice of 2 lemons
a handful of chopped fresh coriander
salt and freshly ground black pepper

1 Mix the yogurt, sweet chilli sauce, garlic, ginger and curry powder in a large bowl.

2 Place the chicken thighs on a chopping board, skin side down, and slash the meat a few times with a sharp knife, before placing them in the bowl with the marinade. Use your hands to mix everything together, massaging the marinade into the chicken. Cover and leave to marinate in the fridge for at least 30 minutes. (Ideally, I do this part of the recipe in the morning so that the chicken marinates all day.)

3 Preheat the oven to 200°C/400°F/gas 6. Place the marinated chicken thighs in a large ovenproof dish. (Make sure the dish isn't overcrowded, or the skins won't crisp up.) Roast for 40–50 minutes, until they're nicely caramelised and crispy.

4 When the chicken is in the oven about 30 minutes, you can start preparing the rice. Put the rice in a jug of cold water, stir, then drain. Repeat this in a few changes of water, then drain the rice in a sieve. Bring a large pan of water to a fast rolling boil and add a good pinch of salt. Add the drained rice, stir once, then boil rapidly without a lid for 6–8 minutes, until the rice is just tender. Drain well and place the rice in a serving dish. Stir in the lemon juice and zest, and coriander. Mix well and season to taste.

5 Serve 2 chicken thighs per person alongside a nice helping of rice.

QUICK BANOFFEE PIE

Buttery biscuits, caramel, bananas and cream... Banoffee pie is a classic dessert full of all things irresistibly naughty. There is nothing difficult about making banoffee but the caramel can be time-consuming. Usually, you boil an unopened can of condensed milk in a saucepan of water for 2 ½ hours, during which it magically turns into caramel.

This version is great for when you don't have 2 ½ hours to spare: the caramel comes together in about 10 minutes. It's a great way to whip together a foolproof pudding in a short time.
Makes a 23 cm pie

For the base
100 g butter
300 g chocolate Hobnob biscuits (Digestives work fine, but I love the oatiness the Hobnobs bring)

For the caramel
100 g butter
100 g brown sugar
1 x 400 g can condensed milk

3 large bananas, peeled and cut into 1 cm rounds
250 ml double cream
grated chocolate, to serve

1 Grease a 23 cm (9 inch) springform cake tin.

2 Melt the butter in a small pan over a low heat. Place the Hobnobs in a food processor and blitz into fine crumbs. Transfer the crumbs to a bowl, pour in the melted butter and stir until combined. Press this mixture firmly and evenly into the base of the cake tin. Place in the fridge to chill for 10 minutes.

3 To make the caramel, melt the butter in a medium saucepan over a low heat. Stir in the sugar, until it dissolves completely. Add the condensed milk. Slowly bring it to the boil, stirring vigorously and continuously. Once boiling point is reached, boil rapidly for 1–2 minutes, until the mixture thickens and turns a light brown colour – and that's it, your caramel is ready! Be careful not to burn the caramel. And it will be extremely hot, so don't be tempted to dip your finger in to taste it.

4 Pour the caramel into the biscuit base and spread it around evenly. Layer the banana slices on top of the caramel and then place the cake tin back in the fridge for at least 30 minutes.

5 When the caramel has cooled, whip the cream until it holds soft peaks. Release the pie from the tin and spread the whipped cream evenly on top. Grate some chocolate over the pie and serve.

LAMB BURGERS WITH TOMATO AND CORIANDER RAITA

These lamb burgers are show stoppers! Any time I've made them for people, they've commented on how tasty the burgers are. You can fry or grill the burgers; and they're lovely on the barbecue, too. I like to serve them in pitta bread but any flatbread would work.

Raita is an Indian condiment, made by mixing yogurt with different seasonings. It can be used as a sauce or dip. This tomato and coriander raita is absolutely perfect with the burgers.
Makes 6–8 burgers

700 g minced lamb
2 garlic cloves, crushed
a thumb-sized piece of ginger, grated
1 small onion, finely chopped
1 red chilli, deseeded and finely chopped
3 teaspoons curry powder
salt and freshly ground black pepper
1 egg, beaten
olive oil
pitta breads, to serve

For the raita
5 tomatoes, halved
250 g Greek yogurt
a handful of fresh chopped coriander
a squeeze of lime juice

1 Place the minced lamb, garlic, ginger, onion, chilli and curry powder in a large bowl and stir to combine. Season and add the egg. Mix with your hands to combine everything thoroughly. Shape the mixture into 6–8 burgers. Cover and refrigerate the burgers for at least 30 minutes.

2 Meanwhile, make the raita. Scoop out the tomatoes, discard the seeds and chop the tomato flesh into small dice. Place the diced tomatoes in a bowl with the yogurt, coriander and lime juice and mix well.

3 Heat a large frying pan over a high heat. Rub the burgers lightly with olive oil and cook for 5–6 minutes each side for medium (7–8 minutes each side for well done). You might need to cook them in batches.

4 Lightly toast the pitta breads. Split open and stuff with the burgers and a dollop of raita. The pitta burgers are lovely by themselves but they're great with the Rosemary Chips on p.27, too.

RASPBERRY SMOOTHIES

Smoothies are a great option for breakfast on the go and they also make a really refreshing dessert or snack. They take virtually no time to put together. I often make a smoothie in the afternoon to give me a kick-start. Summer berries work really well in smoothies. The raspberries in this one make it delicious – the fact that it's healthy is an added bonus. **Serves 4**

160 g raspberries (fresh or frozen work fine)
2 ripe bananas
250 ml milk
250 g natural yogurt
1 teaspoon vanilla extract
1 tablespoon honey

Put everything into a food processor or blender and blitz until smooth. Taste and add more honey if needs be. Pour into glasses and serve. Super simple, super tasty!

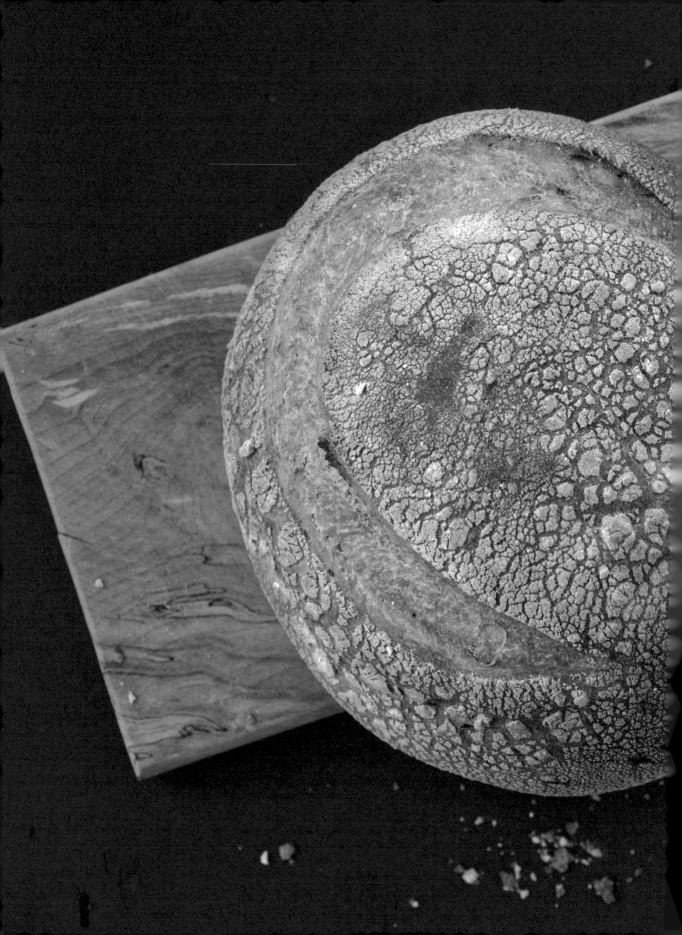

THERE'S NOT MUCH TIME LEFT TO GET THE BARBECUE OUT, SO IF IT HASN'T MADE AN APPEARANCE BY AUGUST, I MAKE SURE TO BRING IT OUT THEN, EVEN IF IT'S NOT THAT WARM. AND LET'S FACE IT, WE CAN'T BE TOO PICKY IN IRELAND WHEN IT COMES TO WEATHER! BARBECUES ARE A GREAT EXCUSE TO GET SOME FRIENDS AROUND AT THE WEEKEND, AND TO PICK AT LOTS OF DELICIOUS MARI-NATED MEATS AND SUMMER SALADS ALL DAY LONG WHILE CHATTING WELL INTO THE NIGHT...

AUGUST

CRUNCHY BLT SALAD

What could be better than a salad made with all the wonderful things from a classic BLT sandwich? I'm definitely not one for boring, insubstantial salads and this salad is testament to that. It's packed with crispy bacon and croutons, tossed in a tangy mayonnaise dressing. I could happily eat this salad several times a week! **Serves 4**

For the dressing
3 tablespoons mayonnaise
2 tablespoons white wine vinegar
juice of ½ lemon
10 g fresh basil leaves, finely chopped
salt and freshly ground black pepper

220 g French stick or any white bread, cut into 2 cm cubes
olive oil
8–10 slices bacon
2 cos lettuces (about 450 g), coarsely chopped
450 g cherry tomatoes, halved

1 Preheat the oven to 180°C/350°F/gas 4.

2 Use a balloon whisk to mix all the dressing ingredients in a bowl. Season and set aside.

3 Toss the bread cubes in a little olive oil in an ovenproof dish. Bake them for 10–15 minutes, until golden, turning once during cooking. Keep a close eye so that they don't burn.

4 Meanwhile, fry the bacon slices in a large frying pan over a high heat, until crispy. Cut the cooked bacon into bite-sized pieces.

5 Mix the cos lettuce, bacon, tomatoes and croutons in a large serving bowl. Pour over just enough dressing to lightly coat the salad. Toss well and serve immediately.

ITALIAN TOMATO AND BREAD SALAD

You'll love this simple summer starter. It's a wonderfully colourful salad, full of vibrant flavours and great textures. It's a favourite in Italy, where they call it Panzanella. You must use good, ripe tomatoes to make this salad the best it can be. **Serves 4**

200 g ciabatta, torn into bite-sized pieces
2 cloves garlic, finely chopped
salt and freshly ground black pepper
olive oil
600 g tomatoes, sliced
a handful of pitted green olives, halved
balsamic vinegar
a large bunch of fresh basil leaves, torn

1 Preheat the oven to 180°C/350°F/gas 4.

2 Place the ciabatta pieces and garlic in an ovenproof dish. Season and add a few tablespoons of olive oil, tossing to coat everything well. Bake for 10–15 minutes, until golden, turning once during cooking. Keep a close eye so that they don't burn.

3 Place the tomato slices in a large serving bowl, along with the olives and cooked ciabatta pieces. Season and mix well with your hands. Stir in 2 tablespoons of balsamic vinegar and 4 tablespoons of olive oil. Taste and tweak to your liking.

4 Sprinkle the basil over the salad, stir once more and serve immediately so the ciabatta pieces stay crunchy.

ITALIAN TOMATO AND BREAD SALAD

CRUNCHY BLT SALAD

LEMONY PLUM CAKE

This cake is scrumptiously moist and so easy to make! It is particularly nice in the late summer months when good, juicy plums are available. **Serves 8**

190 g plain flour, plus extra for dusting
1/4 teaspoon salt
1/2 teaspoon bread soda (bicarbonate of soda)
170 g unsalted butter, at room temperature
100 g brown sugar
110 g caster sugar
3 eggs, beaten
1 teaspoon vanilla extract
2 1/2 teaspoons finely grated lemon zest
85 g natural yogurt
3 plums, stoned and sliced thickly

1 Preheat the oven to 180°C/350°F/ gas 4. Grease a 23 cm (9 inch) springform cake tin and line the base with parchment paper.

2 Sift the flour, salt and bread soda in a bowl and set aside.

3 Cream the butter and sugars in a large bowl with an electric beater, until light and fluffy. Gradually beat in the eggs until well combined. Beat in the vanilla extract and lemon zest. With the mixer on low, beat in half the flour mixture. Then beat in the yogurt until combined. Finally, beat in the second half of the flour mixture and mix until just combined.

4 Pour the batter into the cake tin, smoothing the top. Dust the plum slices with a little flour, then arrange them in a nice pattern on top of the cake batter. Bake for 30 minutes, until the cake is golden. Then loosely cover the tin with tin foil and bake for a further 30–35 minutes, until the cake is coming away from the sides of the tin and a skewer inserted into the centre comes out clean.

5 Allow the cake to cool completely. Then release it from the tin, cut it into slices and serve with a dollop of plain yogurt.

BAKED LAMB WITH TOMATOES AND AUBERGINE

I love cooking meals where you just chuck everything into a baking dish and then throw it in the oven to do its thing – it always feels so effortless and satisfying after a long and tiring day.

Aubergine and lamb go really well together and the tomatoes are also a great addition here. This tasty dish is quite filling. You could serve it with plain boiled potatoes or the Roast Baby Potatoes on p.15, putting them in the oven at the same time as the lamb. **Serves 4**

olive oil
2 onions, roughly chopped
2 aubergines, halved and cut into 2 cm pieces
2 garlic cloves, chopped
1 teaspoon dried oregano
8 ripe plum tomatoes, roughly chopped
salt and freshly ground black pepper
a small handful of fresh basil, torn
8 lamb loin chops, trimmed of excess fat

1 Preheat the oven to 180°C/350°F/gas 4.

2 Heat a few lugs of olive oil in a large frying pan over a medium heat. Add the onions and fry for about 5 minutes, until softened. Add the aubergine pieces and fry until they start to colour. Add the garlic, oregano and tomatoes and cook for another 5 minutes. Season to taste.

3 Transfer the contents of the pan to a shallow ovenproof dish. Sprinkle over the basil and place the lamb chops on top. Drizzle the chops with a little olive oil, season, and roast for 15–20 minutes (depending on thickness of the chops) to keep a little pinkness inside the lamb.

4 Divide the chops among warmed plates, spoon some of the lovely vegetables on top and serve.

STICKY, TANGY CHICKEN WINGS

For years, my friends and I have been obsessed with the famous chicken wings from Elephant & Castle in Dublin's Temple Bar. As soon as you walk in the restaurant, you're hit with that amazing smell of the sauce wafting through the place. I haven't tried to imitate E&C's sauce because if I started making the wings at home it would take the excitement out of going there with my mates. Some things should just be left untouched!

However, this recipe does make delicious chicken wings. The sauce is sweet, spicy and tangy all at the same time, with a lovely stickiness that means you just can't resist licking your fingers – but that's all part of the fun! The wings are lovely served with plain rice and a simple green salad.
Serves 4

olive oil
2 cloves garlic, crushed
6 tablespoons honey
180 g tomato ketchup
100 ml Worcestershire sauce
1 tablespoon Tabasco sauce
1 tablespoon Dijon mustard
3–4 tablespoons plain flour
salt and freshly ground black pepper
24 chicken wings

1 Preheat the oven to 200°C/400°F/gas 6.

2 Heat a lug of olive oil in a small pan over a low heat. Add the garlic and cook for 30 seconds. Add the honey, ketchup, Worcestershire sauce, Tabasco sauce and mustard. Stir well and slowly bring to the boil. Simmer gently for 3–4 minutes, then remove from the heat.

3 Place the flour and some seasoning in a large bowl. Lightly dust the chicken wings in the flour, then arrange them in a single layer in an ovenproof dish. They shouldn't be over-crowded, so use two dishes if necessary.

4 Pour the sauce over the wings and toss them around to coat evenly. Roast for 45–60 minutes, basting halfway through, until the wings are well browned and sticky.

5 Serve – and expect to get messy fingers!

ALMOND BAKED PEACHES WITH WHITE CHOCOLATE SAUCE

This is a variation on a dessert I learned to make during a cookery course in Toffia, Italy. I would say it's in my top five summer desserts – it's that good! I remember making it for my dad on his birthday years ago and he still goes on about it! The combination of peach and almond with a drizzle of white chocolate sauce is absolutely to die for... Serves 6

7 very ripe peaches, cut into 14 halves and stoned
2 tablespoons caster sugar
85 g ground almonds
grated zest of 1 lemon
grated zest of ½ orange
1 egg yolk
30 g butter, melted
a large bar of white chocolate, roughly chopped

1 Preheat the oven to 180°C/350°F/gas 4.

2 Take 2 peach halves and scoop out all their flesh into a large bowl. Discard the skins. For the 12 remaining peach halves, scoop out some (not all) of their flesh and place it in the same large bowl. Arrange the 12 peach skins snugly in an ovenproof dish, hollow side up.

3 Mix the peach flesh in the bowl until it resembles a purée. Add the sugar, almonds, lemon and orange zest, egg yolk and melted butter and mix well.

4 Use a spoon to divide the almond peach filling among the peach halves in the oven dish. Bake for 40–45 minutes, until nicely browned.

5 A few minutes before the peaches are done, melt the white chocolate in a heatproof bowl over a pan of simmering water.

6 To serve, spoon a few tablespoons of the melted chocolate onto each serving plate and place 2 peach halves on top. Delish!

HOMEMADE THIN-CRUST PIZZAS

I enjoy making pizza as much as I enjoy eating pizza! It's a fun way to spend time with family and friends. You might think that making pizza is not worth the effort when frozen and takeaway versions are so readily available, but homemade pizza is so much healthier and fresh ingredients have much more flavour.

I actually use tortilla wraps as pizza bases; they make a lovely thin and crispy crust. This is much quicker than making pizza dough, so it's perfect for a midweek meal. However, pizza dough is easy to make, so give it a go some time!

If you don't like the sound of homemade pizza dough or tortilla bases, you can use shop-bought pizza bases. And if you don't want to make the sauce, a jar of passata works fine. Either way, have fun experimenting with lots of different fresh toppings. This is my top meal for having a laugh with friends. Try it yourself and have fun! **Makes 4 pizzas**

olive oil
1 red onion, thinly sliced
1 red pepper, thinly sliced
1 yellow pepper, thinly sliced
2 x 400 g tins chopped tomatoes
salt and freshly ground black pepper
sugar
8 large tortilla wraps
a handful of fresh basil leaves
100 g chorizo sausage, sliced into 1 cm rounds
4 x 150 g mozzarella balls, torn
1 red chilli, finely sliced
4 slices Parma ham, roughly torn
a handful of rocket leaves

1 Preheat the oven to 220°C/425°F/gas 7.

2 First make the pizza sauce. Heat a lug of olive oil in a large saucepan over a medium heat. Add the onion and fry for 5 minutes, until softened. Add the peppers and fry for another few minutes. Add the tomatoes, seasoning and a pinch of sugar, and stir. Gently simmer the sauce for about 10 minutes, until reduced.

3 Now comes the fun bit: putting your pizzas together. I've given two different suggestions for toppings here, but go with whatever suits your taste. The key is not to overload the pizzas with toppings, or the bases won't crisp up.

4 To create each pizza base, place two tortilla wraps (one on top of the other) on a pizza pan. Each pizza base needs a separate pizza pan. If you don't have pizza pans, use upturned roasting tins; just make sure there's enough room for each pizza to lie completely flat. Using two wraps stuck together

like this makes each pizza base more stable and means it won't collapse as you're eating it.

5 Assemble the first two pizzas. Smear some pizza sauce over each base. Place a few basil leaves and some chorizo slices on top. Make sure the chorizo is uncovered so that it crisps up. Dot mozzarella pieces in any free space. Place the pizzas in the oven and cook for 10 minutes, until golden and bubbling.

6 While the first two pizzas are in the oven, assemble the next two in much the same way. Smear sauce on each pizza base and dot around some mozzarella pieces. Add as many chilli slices as you like and season. Finally, top with the Parma ham, which will crisp beautifully in the oven.

7 As soon as the first two pizzas are ready, take them out of the oven and put the second two straight in. (Don't leave your oven open or you'll lose heat.) Tuck into the cooked pizzas while the other pizzas are in the oven. As soon as you've finished eating the first batch, the second batch will be ready! Top the second batch with rocket leaves before serving.

BLUEBERRY CRUMBLE CAKES

These little cake squares are so simple to make, you can't go wrong. Blueberries are gorgeous in late summer and I love the blueberry-lemony flavour of these baked treats. The buttery, crumbly topping is divine, too.

The cakes make a great afternoon snack with a cup of tea, but they're also lovely as a dessert with some vanilla ice cream. They will keep well in the fridge for 4–5 days.

Makes about 25 squares (but you can cut them as big or as small as you like)

For the crumble
380 g plain flour
225 g sugar
finely grated zest and juice of 1 lemon, divided
1 teaspoon baking powder
salt
225 g cold butter, cubed
1 egg, lightly beaten
1 teaspoon vanilla extract

For the blueberries
110 g sugar
1 tablespoon cornflour
500 g blueberries

1 Preheat the oven to 180°C/350°F/gas 4. Grease and line a 20 cm (8 inch) square tin with baking parchment.

2 Place the flour, sugar, lemon zest (leaving the juice aside for now), baking powder and a pinch of salt in a food processor. Add the butter and blitz to combine. Add the egg and vanilla extract and blitz to form a crumbly dough. Do not overwork the dough; it should be crumbly.

3 Take half the dough and use your hands to press it into the base of the prepared baking tin. Set aside.

4 Stir the 110 g sugar, cornflour and lemon juice together in a large bowl. Gently stir in the blueberries. Pour this blueberry mixture over the dough base in the baking tin, spreading it evenly.

5 Now take the remaining half of the dough and crumble it over the blueberries. You don't need to press this dough together; it's nicer left as a crumbly topping. Bake for 40–45 minutes or until the topping is golden.

6 Leave the cake to cool before you cut it into squares and serve.

IT'S THAT BACK-TO-SCHOOL TIME OF YEAR AND THE SHOPS ARE BUZZING. IT CAN BE A HECTIC TIME, BUT WHAT I LOVE AROUND NOW IS THE TRANSFORMATION OF THE GREEN COLOURS OF SUMMER INTO THE VIVID AUTUMN PALETTE OF REDS, ORANGES, GOLDS AND BROWNS, BEFORE THE LEAVES FALL FROM THE TREES... BEAUTIFUL. SEPTEMBER ALSO BRINGS BIRTHDAYS FOR ME AND A FEW OF MY GIRLFRIENDS, WHICH MEANS LOTS OF CAKE AND PARTIES – FUN!

SEP TEM BER

DAD'S CHINESE BEEF

I've mentioned my mum a bit in this book but it must be said that my dad is a very good cook, too. My granny taught him – and she was a legend in the kitchen. When I think of my dad cooking, it's this dish that comes to mind. It's so delicious that I used to ask him to make it for me all the time when I was younger.

Recently, dad told me the story of where he got this recipe. In the seventies, he went to New York as a student. It was there that he found a gem Szechuan restaurant that served this gorgeous Chinese beef dish. There weren't many Chinese restaurants in Ireland in the seventies, so dad fell in love with this dish and even got the recipe from the chef in New York! Over the years, he modified the recipe to make it his own.

It's best to have all the ingredients prepped before you start this recipe, as it moves quickly! Serves 4

8 tablespoons soy sauce (preferably dark)
6 tablespoons white wine (Chinese rice wine also works well)
4 teaspoons caster sugar
700 g sirloin steak, cut into thin strips
olive oil
2 carrots, cut into long, very thin strips
2 celery sticks, cut into long, very thin strips
2 teaspoons ginger, peeled and finely chopped
6 dried red chillies, finely chopped (use fewer chillies if you don't want it too hot)

1 Mix the soy sauce, white wine and sugar in a medium bowl. Add the steak strips and mix well. Cover and leave to marinate in the fridge for at least 30 minutes.

2 While the beef is marinating, prepare the Fluffy Rice on p.58 and leave it in the oven until ready to serve.

3 Heat a few lugs of olive oil in a large frying pan or wok over a high heat. When the pan is very hot, add the carrot and celery and stir-fry for 90 seconds, then remove to a bowl.

4 If the pan seems too dry, add a little olive oil and wait for it to reach a high heat. Add the ginger and chillies and stir-fry for just 10 seconds.

5 Pour the steak and its marinade into the pan and stir-fry for 4–5 minutes. Return the carrot and celery to the pan, stir-fry for 1 minute – and everything's done! Serve on warmed plates with generous portions of rice.

GRILLED PINEAPPLE WITH LEMON AND VANILLA MASCARPONE

This is a wonderful, super-speedy dessert. We often get great weather in September and if it's nice outside, these pineapples would be great done on the barbecue. The sweetened, creamy mascarpone is delicious with the pineapples but ice cream or crème fraîche would be just as lovely.
Serves 4

1 large ripe pineapple
icing sugar, for dusting
250 g mascarpone
1 teaspoon vanilla extract
1 heaped tablespoon caster sugar
grated zest and juice of 1 lemon

1 Preheat the grill or barbecue.

2 Slice the top and bottom off the pineapple, sit it upright on a board and slice away the skin and all the little brown 'eyes'. Slice the pineapple into thin rounds, cutting away any sharp edges.

3 Dust the pineapple slices with icing sugar and place them on a wire rack directly under the grill. Grill for about 3 minutes on each side, until the fruit is hot and juicy.

4 Meanwhile, mix the mascarpone, vanilla extract, caster sugar, lemon zest and juice in a medium bowl until well combined.

5 Divide the grilled pineapple slices among plates and serve with a generous dollop of sweetened mascarpone on top.

STUFFED PORK TENDERLOIN WRAPPED IN PARMA HAM WITH BUTTERED LEEKS

Pork tenderloin is great for stuffing and popping in the oven. It doesn't take too long to cook and it's a really good value cut of meat. Since it's so tasty and easy to prepare, I tend to eat it a lot. Wrapping tenderloin in Parma ham (or another cured ham) is lovely because the crisp saltiness goes really well with the meat and also keeps it nice and moist. Buttered leeks are a lovely accompaniment to this pork dish, as is the Mustard Mash on p.11. **Serves 4**

butter
½ onion, finely chopped
80 g breadcrumbs
25 g finely chopped fresh parsley
25 g finely chopped fresh rosemary
salt and freshly ground black pepper
2 tenderloin pork fillets (about 350 g each) or 1 large fillet cut in half
8 slices Parma ham
4–6 leeks, washed, trimmed and cut into 5 mm rounds

1 Preheat the oven to 200°C/400°F/gas 6.

2 First make the stuffing. Melt a knob of butter in a medium saucepan over a gentle heat. Add the onion and sauté for 4–5 minutes, until softened but not coloured. Add the breadcrumbs, parsley and rosemary, and stir to combine. Season and set aside.

3 Lay the pork fillets on a chopping board and trim off any excess fat. Using a sharp knife, slit open each fillet from the side, as you would a pitta bread. Don't cut all the way through: you just want to open out the fillet so you can stuff it. Bash the meat a little with your fists to thin it out, then season with a little salt and lots of black pepper.

4 Stuff the fillets with the breadcrumb mixture, then fold over to enclose. Lay 4 Parma slices on the chopping board and arrange so that they overlap slightly; repeat with the remaining 4 slices. Place each fillet on top of 4 Parma slices and wrap the fillet in the Parma to completely seal it. Tie the pork parcels with string at 3 cm intervals, if they need extra securing.

5 Place the pork parcels in an ovenproof dish and roast for 35–40 minutes, until the ham is crispy and the meat is cooked through.

6 Meanwhile, cook the leeks. Melt a knob of butter in a large saucepan over a medium heat. Toss the leeks in the butter, season and cook for 15–20 minutes, until very soft. Stir occasionally to prevent the leeks over-browning.

7 Remove the pork from the oven and leave to rest for 5 minutes. Divide the leeks between warmed serving plates. Slice the pork fillets, arrange them on top of the leeks and serve.

ASIAN MANGO SALAD

This is such a colourful salad and it looks really gorgeous on the plate. It's a great starter to pair with an Asian main course, as it leaves you wanting more of those yummy Asian flavours. The crunchy, sweet, tangy, spicy combination in this salad is simply amazing. Serves 4

For the dressing
juice of 2 limes
1 tablespoon olive oil
1 teaspoon brown sugar
1 red chilli, deseeded and finely chopped
a handful of fresh coriander, roughly chopped

75 g raw cashew nuts
2 ripe mangos, peeled and cut into thin strips
a handful of French beans, tailed and halved lengthways
1 red pepper, finely sliced
½ red onion, finely sliced
a handful of mint leaves, roughly chopped

1 Place all the ingredients for the dressing in a small bowl. Add a pinch of salt. Mix well and set aside.

2 Heat a small pan over a medium heat and add the cashews. Toast them for a few minutes, tossing regularly, until golden. Remove the cashews from the pan, leave them to cool, then roughly chop them.

3 Place the mango, French beans, pepper and onion in a serving bowl. Pour over the dressing and toss well to coat evenly. Just before serving, sprinkle over the mint and cashews.

CHICKEN LAKSA

Laksa is a coconut-based soup with noodles. It's a great example of how fresh and clean Asian flavours can be. I just love the combination of lime, coriander, coconut and chilli in this soup; it's like a hug in a bowl! This meal is very healthy and also easy and quick to prepare – what could be better? **Serves 4**

600 ml chicken stock, simmering
a thumb-sized piece of ginger, peeled and finely sliced
3 chicken breasts, cut into thin strips
juice of 2 limes
200 ml coconut milk
a few handfuls of baby spinach leaves
2 nests of fine rice noodles or egg noodles
2 red chillies, deseeded and finely chopped (use just 1 if you prefer less heat)
a large handful of fresh coriander, roughly chopped

1 Place the chicken stock and ginger in a large pan over a high heat. Bring to the boil and add the chicken strips, lime juice and coconut milk and stir well. Cook over a high heat for about 5 minutes, until the chicken is just cooked. Stir in the spinach leaves and cook until the spinach wilts.

2 Meanwhile, cook the noodles in a large pan of boiling salted water, according to packet instructions. Drain the cooked noodles and stir them into the Laksa when the spinach has wilted.

3 Add the chilli and coriander, give it a quick stir, then serve immediately in warmed bowls.

SAUSAGE, MUSHROOM AND TOMATO PASTA

This is an express home-cooked meal – easy, quick and extremely tasty! It's really worth using the best-quality sausages you can find for this dish, otherwise it could really disappoint. **Serves 4**

olive oil
6 thick, good-quality pork sausages, cut into bite-sized pieces
250 g mushrooms, thinly sliced, divided
salt and freshly ground black pepper
2 garlic cloves, crushed
200 ml white wine
1 x 400 g can chopped tomatoes
1 tablespoon tomato purée
500 g rigatoni, fusilli or penne pasta
a handful of basil leaves, torn

1 Heat a lug of olive oil in a large pan over a medium-high heat. Fry the sausage pieces for 6–8 minutes, until golden and cooked through. Use a slotted spoon to transfer the sausages to a bowl. Discard any excess oil from the frying pan.

2 Turn the heat to high and add half the mushrooms to the pan. Season and fry for 3–4 minutes, until brown. Transfer the mushrooms to the bowl with the sausages.

3 Add another lug of olive oil to the pan and fry the remaining mushrooms, as before. Return the sausage and mushroom mixture to the pan. Add the garlic and cook for 1 minute. Stir in the wine and cook for about 4 minutes, until the wine has reduced by half.

4 Add the tomatoes, tomato purée and seasoning. Simmer for 8–10 minutes, until reduced to a nice consistency.

5 Meanwhile, cook the pasta in a large pan of boiling salted water, according to packet instructions. Always cook pasta in a large volume of water. The Italians say the water should be as salty as sea water, so use plenty of salt and you won't have to season after cooking. Cook the pasta until al dente (tender but firm to the bite).

6 Drain the pasta, keeping back a few tablespoons of the cooking water. Return the pasta to its pan and stir with the cooking water. This will help to loosen the pasta and retain the seasoning.

7 Add the sausage and mushroom sauce to the cooked pasta and stir well to combine. Stir in the torn basil leaves and serve immediately in warmed bowls.

BLONDIES

If it looks a bit like a brownie, it could be a blondie! A blondie is essentially a brownie without the chocolate and there are many different variations. Some have fruit, oats or nuts, but my favourite is this one with white chocolate and pecans. It's an absolute dream with a cup of tea!
Makes about 9 squares

150 g butter
150 g caster sugar
1 teaspoon vanilla extract
2 eggs
120 g plain flour, sieved
80 g pecan nuts, chopped
150 g white chocolate, roughly chopped

1 Preheat the oven to 180°C/350°F/gas 4. Grease a 16 cm (6 inch) square tin and line it with parchment paper.

2 Melt the butter in a small pan over a low heat.

3 Whisk the sugar, vanilla extract and eggs in a large bowl with an electric beater, until pale and fluffy. Beat in the melted butter, a little at a time, until fully incorporated. Carefully fold in the flour. Add the pecans and chocolate and stir until combined.

4 Spoon the mixture into the prepared baking tin and give it a little shake to even it out. Bake for 25–35 minutes or until firm in the centre and a skewer inserted comes out clean.

5 Leave to cool completely in the tin before cutting into squares.

GRILLED COURGETTE AND FETA SALAD

This is a lovely simple salad. I like it as a starter but it's also a great side dish with grilled white fish or cold roast meats. I love how the thinly sliced courgettes work with the crumbly, milky feta. Mmmm...

Courgettes are good in September. Seek out ones that are small and firm; they taste best.
Serves 4

For the dressing
finely grated zest and juice of I lemon
2 tablespoons olive oil
½ clove garlic, finely chopped

4 courgettes
200 g feta, cubed
a handful of basil leaves, torn
a handful of mint leaves, torn

1 Place all the ingredients for the dressing in a small bowl. Add a good grinding of black pepper. Mix and set aside.

2 Use a potato peeler to peel the courgettes lengthways into very thin slices. Heat a grill pan or frying pan over a high heat and cook the courgette slices for a few minutes on each side, until slightly charred. (You might need to do them in batches.)

3 Arrange the charred courgette slices in a single layer on a large serving plate. Scatter the feta cubes over the courgettes, then sprinkle over the basil and mint. Drizzle the dressing evenly over the salad and serve immediately.

OCTOBER BRINGS HALLOWEEN –
A GREAT TIME TO LET YOUR
IMAGINATION RUN WILD. I LOVE
SEEING BRILLIANT COSTUMES AND
AMAZINGLY DETAILED CARVED
PUMPKINS ON WINDOWSILLS, THE
CANDLES INSIDE THEM FLICKER-
ING TO CREATE THAT SPOOKY
ATMOSPHERE THAT BELONGS ONLY
TO THIS TIME OF YEAR... OCTO-
BER IS DEFINITELY THE MONTH TO
GET CARRIED AWAY IN MYSTERY,
FANTASY AND FUN.

OCT OBER

GRANDPA'S FAMOUS FISH CAKES

My mum taught me this fish cake recipe, which her father once taught her. Grandpa was famous in our family for these fish cakes. They contain no potato; instead, they are bound together with a stiff béchamel sauce. They're gorgeous – by far the best fish cake recipe I've ever tried. I hope you like them as much as I do. Serves 4

For the sauce
a few slices of onion
a few slices of carrot
1 bay leaf (or a few sprigs of parsley or thyme)
4 black peppercorns
300 ml milk
450 g white fish fillets, skinned and pinboned
30 g butter, plus extra for frying
30 g flour
1 teaspoon paprika

For the coating
4–5 tablespoons plain flour, seasoned
2 eggs, lightly beaten
200 g breadcrumbs

sunflower oil

1 Place the onion, carrot, bay leaf, peppercorns and milk in a large pan. Add the fish fillets. Bring to the boil, then reduce the heat and simmer for about 5 minutes, until the fish turns opaque. Use a slotted spoon to remove the fish to a plate, then flake it into pieces with a fork.

2 Strain the milk through a sieve over a bowl. Discard the contents of the sieve and set aside the milk for now.

3 Melt the butter in a large pan over a low heat. Stir in the flour. Cook for 2 minutes, stirring all the time, then remove from the heat.

4 Gradually add the strained milk to the butter and flour mixture, blending until smooth. Return the pan to the heat and whisk continuously until boiling. Allow it to bubble for 4–5 minutes, until it thickens to make a very stiff béchamel sauce. Remove from the heat.

5 Add the flaked fish to the pan with the sauce. Season, add the paprika and stir well to combine. Use your hands to shape the mixture into medium-sized cakes and place them in the fridge for 30–60 minutes, until well chilled.

6 Place the seasoned flour, eggs and breadcrumbs in separate bowls. Remove the fish cakes from the fridge and coat each one in flour, then egg, then breadcrumbs.

7 Heat a lug of sunflower oil and a knob of butter in a frying pan over a medium heat. When the butter foams, fry the fish cakes for 3–4 minutes each side, until golden. (You might need to do this in batches.)

8 Divide the fish cakes onto warmed serving plates. Serve them piping hot with a simple green salad or the Pepper Ratatouille on p.27.

HAZELNUT SWIRL COOKIES

At Kooky Dough, we spend a lot of time experimenting with fun recipes using cookie dough. It's such a versatile ingredient and you can use it to make some really extravagant baked treats and desserts.

This recipe is probably my favourite thing to do with cookie dough. The Nutella oozes out of the warm cookies and they're just irresistible! The cookies are super-quick to make if you cheat and use ready-made cookie dough; but if you want to make them from scratch, this recipe shows you how.
Makes 10–12 big cookies

300 g plain flour
¼ teaspoon salt
½ teaspoon bread soda (bicarbonate of soda)
225 g butter, at room temperature

225 g caster sugar
2 egg yolks
1 teaspoon vanilla extract
a jar of Nutella

1 Sift the flour, salt and bread soda into a bowl.

2 Cream the butter and sugar in a large bowl with an electric beater, until pale and fluffy. Add the egg yolks and vanilla extract and mix until combined. With the mixer on low, add the flour mixture a little at a time, until it's fully combined and the mixture becomes a soft dough.

3 Transfer the dough to a lightly floured board and shape it into a rough square. Wrap it in cling film and refrigerate for about 30 minutes.

4 Preheat the oven to 180°C/350°F/gas 4. Line a few baking sheets with parchment paper.

5 Remove the dough from the fridge, discard the cling film and tip the dough onto a large sheet of lightly floured parchment paper. Lay a fresh sheet of cling film on top of the dough and use a rolling pin to roll the dough into a rough rectangular shape of 1–2cm thickness. If you don't have a rolling pin, you can shape the dough using your hands over the cling film. Once the dough is shaped, discard the cling film.

6 Dip a knife into a mug of hot water, then into the jar of Nutella (this will help loosen the Nutella). Spread Nutella generously on top of the dough, leaving a 1 cm edge untouched all around.

7 Using the parchment underneath the dough as a guide, roll the dough into a tight log (ensuring the parchment paper doesn't catch). Cut the log into 1 cm slices (or thicker if you like).

8 Arrange the cookie dough slices on the lined baking sheets. Ensure they are well spaced, so that they have room to spread out in the oven.

9 Bake for 10–12 minutes, until lightly golden. The Nutella swirls will look amazing at this stage! Leave the cookies to cool on the trays for a few minutes, before transferring them to a wire rack.

10 Enjoy with a cup of tea, or dig out the vanilla ice cream for a yummy dessert!

CHICKEN, LEEK AND BUTTER BEAN SOUP

When it starts to get cold again during the autumn, I begin to crave big, hearty, filling soups. This is one of those soups... It's so warming and soothing, perfect on a windy and rainy evening. The lightly mashed butter beans give the soup a gorgeously creamy texture. It only takes about half an hour to cook and it's a complete meal in itself. The leftovers keep well in the fridge, too.
Makes 4 large portions

olive oil
4 leeks, washed, trimmed and cut into 5mm rounds
2 garlic cloves, crushed
2 celery sticks, finely chopped
4 chicken breasts, cut into thin strips
1 litre chicken stock, simmering
2 x 400 g cans butter beans, rinsed, drained and mashed lightly
2 tablespoons Dijon mustard
finely grated zest of 2 lemons
2 tablespoons chopped fresh parsley
salt and freshly ground black pepper
50 ml Greek yogurt or crème fraîche (optional)

1 Heat a few lugs of olive oil in a large pan over a low-medium heat. Add the leeks, garlic and celery and fry for about 10 minutes, until soft.

2 Add the chicken, increase the heat and fry for 2–3 minutes. Add the chicken stock and butter beans and bring to a simmer. Now add the mustard, lemon zest, parsley and plenty of seasoning. Stir well and cook for about 15 minutes, until the chicken is fully cooked.

3 Stir in the yogurt or crème fraîche, if using. Serve in big warmed bowls with a helping of crusty bread on the side.

OATY BLACKBERRY AND APPLE CRUMBLE

Crumbles are a classic dessert for a reason – you just can't beat a serving of crumble served hot from the oven with some cream or ice cream melting on top! They're fantastic for a midweek dessert because they're so simple to make.

Traditional crumble topping is made with flour, butter and sugar, but I love the crunchiness that the oats add to this crumble. The addition of some chopped nuts would be lovely, too. **Serves 6–8**

650 g Bramley cooking apples (about 3 apples), peeled, cored and cut into 2 cm cubes
300 g blackberries
30 g sugar
100 g plain flour
150 g porridge oats
100 g cold butter, cubed (preferably unsalted)
75 g brown sugar
vanilla ice cream or pouring cream, to serve

1 Preheat the oven to 180°C/350°F/gas 4. Grease a large, shallow ovenproof dish.

2 Place the apple pieces, blackberries and 30 g sugar in a large bowl and use your hands to toss everything together. Transfer this mixture to the prepared dish.

3 Place the flour, oats and butter in another large bowl and rub this mixture with your fingertips until it resembles crumbs. Stir in the brown sugar.

4 Pour the crumble mixture evenly over the fruit in the ovenproof dish. Bake for 45–50 minutes, until the crumble is light golden, the blackberries are oozing and the apples are completely soft.

5 Serve hot with vanilla ice cream or cream.

SPICY HUMMUS WITH PITTA

I'm completely addicted to hummus. I could easily sit in front of a bowl of it and devour the whole thing in no time! You can buy it easily in supermarkets but this homemade version is so handy and actually much cheaper than shop-bought stuff.

This isn't a traditional hummus: it doesn't have tahini in it. Tahini is a sesame seed paste and I find it quite rich, so I usually leave it out. I love the spicy kick that the cayenne adds to this recipe, but you can omit it if you wish.

Hummus is really versatile and it makes a wonderful starter when served with toasted pitta bread. Any leftovers from this recipe will last in the fridge for 4–5 days. Serves 4

1 x 400 g can chickpeas, rinsed and drained
2 garlic cloves, crushed
juice of ½–1 lemon, according to taste
1 teaspoon paprika, plus extra for garnishing
1 teaspoon cayenne pepper (optional)
olive oil
salt
a small handful of fresh coriander
pitta breads, to serve

1 Place the chickpeas, garlic, lemon juice, paprika and cayenne pepper, if using, in a food processor and blitz until finely chopped.

2 With the food processor on low, pour 3 tablespoons of olive oil through the spout in a slow stream until blended to a nice, smooth consistency. If you want to make it even smoother, add a little more olive oil, lemon juice or both.

3 Add a pinch of salt and blitz again. Taste and add more salt if needs be. Add the coriander and briefly blitz one more time, until the coriander is mixed through.

4 Lightly toast the pitta breads and cut them into wedges. Scrape the hummus into a serving bowl, drizzle with olive oil and sprinkle a little paprika on top. Enjoy!

CURRIED LAMB WITH CORIANDER AND SWEET POTATO MASH

This dish is made with lamb loin chops. Curry and lamb always make a great combination. The sweet potato mash is a nice change from regular mash; the coriander and lime flavours are what make it particularly delicious. **Serves 4**

a thumb-sized piece of ginger, grated
3 garlic cloves, crushed
juice of 2 limes
4 tablespoons natural yogurt
2 tablespoons curry powder
4 large lamb loin chops (8 if they're small)
salt and freshly ground black pepper

For the mash
4 large sweet potatoes, peeled and roughly chopped
olive oil
juice of 2 limes
a large handful of chopped fresh coriander

1 Preheat the oven to 200°C/400°F/gas 6.

2 Mix the ginger, garlic, lime juice, yogurt and curry powder in a large bowl. Add the lamb, season, and use your hands to mix everything together, massaging the marinade into the lamb. Cover and leave to marinate in the fridge for at least 30 minutes. (Ideally, I do this part of the recipe in the morning so that the lamb marinates all day.)

3 Place the sweet potatoes on a roasting tray. Add a little olive oil, season and mix well to coat evenly. Roast for 30 minutes, until tender.

4 Meanwhile, heat a large frying pan over a high heat. Remove the lamb chops from the marinade and fry for 4–5 minutes each side for medium (depending on thickness of chops). Place the cooked chops on a sheet of tin foil and wrap it to form a loose but firmly sealed parcel. Leave to rest for 5 minutes.

5 Use a slotted spoon to transfer the sweet potatoes to a dish suitable for mashing. Mash the sweet potatoes with the lime juice and a little drizzle of olive oil. Season to taste and stir in the chopped coriander.

6 Divide the mash among warmed serving plates, arrange the lamb on top and serve.

WHOLEGRAIN MUSTARD SALMON WITH PEA COUSCOUS

This dish is a perfect midweek supper: simple, great-tasting food prepared in about 20 minutes. On top of that, it's a very nutritious and healthy meal. Couscous is a great pairing with fish because they both cook so quickly. Serves 4

For the couscous
olive oil
1 onion, finely chopped
1 garlic clove, crushed
150 g frozen peas
260 ml boiling water
salt and freshly ground black pepper
175 g couscous
1 tablespoon chopped fresh parsley
juice of 1 lemon, divided

2 tablespoons wholegrain mustard
50 g sour cream
4 x 180 g salmon fillets, skin on
lemon wedges, to garnish

1 First make the couscous. Heat a lug of olive oil in a large pan over a medium heat. Add the onion and garlic and cook for 5 minutes, until soft and translucent. Stir in the peas and boiling water. Season and return to the boil. Stir in the couscous and remove the pan from the heat. Cover (with a lid or plate) and set aside until the liquid has absorbed fully. This will only take about 5 minutes, but the couscous will happily sit for 15 minutes while you cook the salmon.

2 Preheat the grill to high. Mix the mustard, sour cream and 2 teaspoons of lemon juice in a bowl. Place the salmon fillets, skin side down, on a grill rack lined with foil. Season the fillets and spread each one with some mustard mixture. Place the grill rack about 10 cm away from the heat source. Grill the salmon fillets for 8–10 minutes (depending on thickness of fillets), until just cooked. Keep an eye on them towards the end to ensure the mustard topping doesn't burn.

3 Uncover the couscous and fluff it up with a fork. Stir in the chopped parsley and a little lemon juice, and season.

4 Divide the salmon fillets and couscous among warmed plates, garnish with lemon wedges and serve.

CRÊPES WITH ORANGE BUTTER SAUCE

These are similar to the French classic crêpes suzette, but without the alcohol. I actually prefer these to crêpes suzette – and they're much cheaper to make, since you don't have to use any liqueur.

I used to think I was a traditional lemon-and-sugar-pancake kind of girl...until I tried orange butter ones. They are quite simply amazing. **Serves 4**

For the crêpes
220 g plain flour
2 tablespoons caster sugar
salt
4 eggs
400 ml whole milk, mixed with 150 ml water
4 tablespoons melted butter, plus extra for the pan

For the sauce
100 g icing sugar, sieved
130 g butter, softened
2 teaspoons finely grated orange zest
juice of 2 large oranges, strained

1 Sift the flour, sugar and a pinch of salt into a large bowl and mix until combined. Make a well in the centre of the flour and break the eggs into it. Use a balloon whisk to mix the eggs and flour mixture, until combined. Add the milk and water mixture, a little at a time, whisking well after each addition. Do this until all the liquid is added and the batter is smooth and covered with bubbles. Add the melted butter and whisk again. Leave the batter in the fridge while you make the orange butter, which will form the basis for the sauce.

2 Cream the icing sugar, butter and orange zest in a medium bowl with an electric beater, until pale and fluffy. Set this orange butter aside for now.

3 Before you cook the crêpes, organise your work space. You'll need a small bowl of melted butter and some kitchen paper, so that you can wipe the pan before cooking each crêpe. You'll also need a hot plate to stack the cooked crêpes on.

4 Heat a 20 cm (8 inch) non-stick pan until very hot. Then reduce the heat, wipe the pan with melted butter and pour in just enough batter to cover the base of the pan. (These crêpes are thinner than regular pancakes.) Quickly swirl the pan to spread the batter and use a spatula to loosen the edge of the crêpe away from the pan.

5 Cook for 1 minute. Use a spatula to lift the edge of the crêpe to see if it's cooked underneath. As soon as it's lightly golden, flip it over and cook for 1 minute on the other side, until it's also lightly golden. Slide the cooked crêpe onto a hot plate.

6 Repeat until all the batter is used up, stacking the cooked crêpes on top of each other. You should end up with about 8 crêpes.

7 When all the crêpes are cooked, melt a dollop of the orange butter in the hot pan. Add a good splash of orange juice and, when the butter foams, place a cooked crêpe in the pan. Swirl the pan to coat the crêpe in the buttery orange sauce. Use a spatula to fold the crêpe in half, then in half again, to make a triangular shape. Slide the crêpe onto a warmed serving plate and hand to the first lucky person!

8 Repeat until all the crêpes have been cooked in the buttery orange sauce.

WINTER IS WELL AND TRULY HERE. IT'S TIME TO CLOSE THE CURTAINS, GET A BLAZING FIRE GOING, CURL UP WITH A MASSIVE MUG OF TEA AND SMILE CONTENTLY AS YOU TUCK INTO A WARMING BAKED GOODIE OR PUDDING. THERE'S SOMETHING SO COMFORTING ABOUT SITTING IN FRONT OF THE FIRE, FEELING LIKE YOU'RE A MILLION MILES AWAY FROM THE HARSH WINTER WEATHER OUTSIDE.

NO
VEM
BER

BEEF AND THYME COBBLER

Beef cobbler is essentially a stew topped with scones and baked, so that when the scones rise, the topping looks like cobble stones! It's pure comfort food and a real crowd-pleaser. I use mince in mine because it cooks quicker. This way, you have a great, hearty dish and you don't have to spend hours cooking a stew. It's also a nice way to cook mince if you're not in the mood for Bolognese or a cottage pie.

This cobbler is great for making in advance. You can prepare it and then freeze it before baking. On the day you want to eat it, just pop it in the oven straight from the freezer, bake for 40 minutes – and that's it! I often spend a Sunday afternoon making freezer fillers like this, especially if I know I've a hectic week ahead of me. The little effort involved is so worth it... **Serves 4**

olive oil
I onion, finely chopped
500 g lean minced beef
2 carrots, finely chopped
200 g mushrooms, sliced
2 tablespoons plain flour
I x 400 g can chopped tomatoes
350 ml beef stock, simmering
salt and freshly ground black pepper

For the cobbler topping
280 g self-raising flour
2 tablespoons finely chopped thyme leaves
280 g runny natural yogurt
water (optional)
milk, for glazing

1 Preheat the oven to 220°C/425°F/gas 7.

2 Heat a lug of olive oil in a large pan over a medium heat. Add the onion and cook for 5 minutes, until softened. Turn up the heat, add the mince and cook until browned, stirring regularly. Add the carrots, mushrooms and flour and cook for 1–2 minutes. Add the tomatoes and stock, season and stir well. Reduce the heat, cover with a lid and simmer gently for about 15 minutes.

3 To make the cobbler topping, sift the flour into a large bowl and stir in the thyme and a good pinch of salt. Make a well in the centre and pour in the yogurt. Use your fingers to stir the mixture in a circular motion, starting from the centre and working outwards to incorporate the flour and make a soft dough. Don't overwork the dough. It should not be sticky or wet but you can add water if you think it's too dry. Add just a little at a time; you'll be surprised how quickly it comes together without much liquid. When the dough comes together, place it on a lightly floured board. Use a rolling pin to roll it to about 1.5 cm thickness. Then cut the dough into rounds using a 6 cm cutter.

4 Transfer the mince mixture to an ovenproof dish. Arrange the dough circles in neat rows on top. Brush the dough with a little milk. Bake at 220°C/425°F/gas 7 for 10 minutes. Then reduce the heat to 180°C/350°F/gas 4 and bake for a further 15–18 minutes, until the scones are risen and golden brown.

5 Bring the cobbler straight to the table and let everyone tuck in.

BANANA BREAD

Banana bread is right up there on my list of favourite baked treats. I adore it as an afternoon snack or even for breakfast on a lazy weekend morning. It's brilliant for using up overripe bananas.

*I make banana bread a lot and I've tried many different recipes, but this is the ultimate one in my view. It's really moist and not overly sweet, with a warming hint of cinnamon. I love eating a slice of this when it's still warm from the oven, either on its own or with a slathering of butter. Enjoy it with a big mug of tea or hot chocolate. **Makes 1 loaf***

240 g plain flour
1 heaped teaspoon baking powder
1 teaspoon cinnamon
120 g caster sugar
salt
1 egg
100 ml sunflower oil
1 teaspoon vanilla extract
3 large (or 4 medium) ripe bananas, peeled and mashed
50 g pecan nuts, chopped (optional)

1 Preheat the oven to 180°C/350°F/ gas 4. Grease a 900 g (2 lb) loaf tin and line it with parchment paper.

2 Sift the flour, baking powder, cinnamon, sugar and a pinch of salt into a large bowl. In a separate bowl, mix together the egg, oil and vanilla extract. Pour this egg mixture into the large bowl with the flour. Add the mashed bananas and pecans, if using. Gently fold everything together, until just combined. Do not over-mix.

3 Pour the mixture into the lined loaf tin and bake for 50 minutes until it's golden brown and a skewer inserted comes out clean. Remove the tin from the oven and leave it to cool for a few minutes before turning the bread out onto a wire rack.

CHICKEN TIKKA MASALA WITH GARLIC AND CORIANDER NAANS

Chicken tikka masala is one of the most popular Indian takeaway dishes, but it probably wouldn't feature on any menu in India! Whatever the debate about its origins, a good tikka masala is just gorgeous. Chicken cooked in flavoursome spices and a creamy tomato sauce is such a lovely combination that it's easy to see why this dish is so loved!

In my view, homemade tikka masala beats any takeaway version hands down; and using a good curry paste makes it a breeze to cook. I've teamed it here with garlic and coriander naans and you could also serve it with the Fluffy Rice on p.58 for a complete feast. This curry freezes really well, so why not make a double batch and freeze any leftovers for another day? **Serves 4**

vegetable oil

2 small onions, finely chopped

I garlic clove, finely chopped

a thumb-sized piece of ginger, grated

I red chilli, deseeded and finely chopped

3 large tablespoons tikka masala curry paste
  (make sure it's not tikka masala curry sauce in a
  jar, it must be tikka masala paste!)

I red pepper, diced

4 chicken breasts, cubed

I x 400 g can chopped tomatoes

salt and freshly ground black pepper

I ¹/₂ tablespoons mango chutney

200 g natural yogurt

For the naans

2 tablespoons olive oil

I garlic clove, crushed

2 large plain naans

a large handful of chopped fresh coriander, divided

1 Heat a few lugs of vegetable oil in a large frying pan over a medium-high heat. Add the onions, garlic, ginger and chilli and fry for 3–4 minutes, until softened. Add the tikka masala paste and red pepper and cook for 3–4 minutes. Add the chicken, stir well to coat it in the paste and cook for 1–2 minutes. Add the tomatoes and 100 ml water, season and stir well. Bring to the boil, then reduce the heat, cover with a lid and simmer gently for 15 minutes, stirring occasionally.

2 If you want to serve the Fluffy Rice on p.58, start preparing that now.

3 When the curry has finished simmering, remove the lid and stir in the mango chutney and yogurt until combined. Taste and season if needs be. Leave the curry at a gentle simmer while you prepare the naans.

4 Preheat the grill on a high heat. Mix the olive oil and garlic in a bowl. Splash the naans with a little water, then spread the garlic oil over them. Place the naans on a wire rack directly under the grill. Grill for 1–2 minutes, until golden, watching them carefully so they don't burn. Remove the naans from the grill and sprinkle some coriander over them.

5 Serve the curry on warmed plates with some naan and rice. Garnish the curry with the remaining coriander.

POACHED PEARS WITH CHOCOLATE SAUCE AND TOASTED HAZELNUTS

Poaching fruit is a really easy way to whip up a gorgeous dessert. I particularly enjoy eating poached pears: when teamed with dark chocolate sauce, they create a simple and elegant dessert.

Tweak the poaching syrup to your liking. You can add spices such as cinnamon or ginger; and red wine is beautiful, too. I like to keep things simple with just some lemon and vanilla.

The toasted hazelnuts add a lovely crunch to this dessert, but feel free to leave them out. **Serves 4**

For the pears
200 g sugar
juice of $1/2$ lemon
1 teaspoon vanilla extract
4 firm pears, peeled, halved and cored

200 ml double cream
200 g dark chocolate, finely chopped
a handful of toasted hazelnuts, chopped (optional)

1 Place the sugar, lemon juice, vanilla extract and 500 ml water in a large, wide pan over a medium heat. Stir until the sugar dissolves, and bring to the boil. Place the pears in the sugar syrup, cut side facing up. (The syrup must completely cover the pears.) Cover with a lid and simmer gently for 20–30 minutes, depending on the ripeness of the pears. They are done when a knife inserted meets no resistance. Remove the pan from the heat and leave the pears to cool in the syrup while you make the chocolate sauce.

2 Place the cream in a medium heatproof bowl over a saucepan of simmering water. Make sure the bottom of the bowl doesn't touch the water. As soon as the cream starts to bubble, add the chopped chocolate. Whisk it quickly and remove from the heat as soon as the chocolate has melted – a matter of seconds.

3 Arrange two pear halves in each serving bowl, pour over the warm chocolate sauce and sprinkle chopped hazelnuts over the top. Serve immediately.

BAKED EGGS WITH PARMA HAM AND CHEESE

Baked eggs are such a simple, elegant little dish and they make a fantastic snack or starter. They're also gorgeous for a relaxed brunch at the weekend. There's so little effort involved in making them that you'll be surprised how good they taste.

The really great thing about them is their versatility: you can keep them simple for those who like their eggs unadorned, or jazz them up for people who like all the trimmings. Things like mushrooms, spinach, tomato and chorizo are great with baked eggs; the list is endless, really.

*This recipe with Parma ham and cheese is one of my favourite variations and you don't need to cook any of the ingredients before adding them to the eggs, so it's super-quick. **Serves 4***

butter, for greasing
4 slices Parma ham, chopped
4 teaspoons finely chopped fresh parsley
4 large eggs
salt and freshly ground black pepper
4 tablespoons finely grated cheese (cheddar, Gruyère or Parmesan)

1 Preheat the oven 180°C/350°F/gas 4.

2 Grease 4 ramekins. Line the base of the ramekins with the Parma ham and sprinkle the parsley on top. Break an egg into each ramekin, season and sprinkle some cheese on top.

3 Place the ramekins in a roasting tin half-filled with hot water. Bake for 9–10 minutes, until the white is just set. This amount of time gives a runny yolk. If you prefer hard egg yolks, bake for 12–14 minutes instead. Either way, be careful not to overcook the eggs. Remember that they continue to cook after you take them out of the oven, so it's best to under-bake them slightly.

4 Serve the baked eggs with a generous helping of hot buttered toast.

SPANISH TAPAS OF PAPRIKA CHICKEN, PATATAS BRAVAS AND CHORIZO IN RED WINE

I absolutely love tapas! For me, sharing all the different little plates of delicious food amongst good friends and family is what meals should be all about. In Spain, tapas mean more than just good food: they represent a whole way of life, which I think is lovely.

This recipe involves three of my favourite tapas dishes. Served together, they easily make up a good main course for each person. They're great with a simple salad of rocket leaves on the side. Serves 4–6

For the paprika chicken
I tablespoon paprika
2 tablespoons olive oil
I garlic clove, crushed
¼ teaspoon cayenne pepper
4 chicken breasts
salt

For the patatas bravas
900 g potatoes, peeled, cut into 4 cm cubes and dried well
2 tablespoons olive oil
I small onion, chopped
I garlic clove, crushed
½ teaspoon chilli flakes or dried chilli, chopped
2 teaspoons paprika
70 ml white wine
I x 400 g can chopped tomatoes
I tablespoon tomato purée
sugar
Tabasco sauce
a handful of fresh parsley, chopped

For the chorizo in red wine
I garlic clove, crushed
280 g chorizo sausage, sliced into 2 cm rounds
150 ml red wine
2 bay leaves

1 Preheat the oven to 200°C/400°F/gas 6.

2 First prepare the chicken. Place the paprika, olive oil, garlic, cayenne pepper, chicken and a good pinch of salt in a large bowl. Use your hands to mix everything together, massaging the spicy mixture into the meat. Set aside while you prepare the other ingredients.

3 Place the potato cubes in an ovenproof dish. Add the olive oil and a good pinch of salt and toss well. Roast in the preheated oven for 40 minutes, until golden, turning once during cooking.

4 To make the sauce for the patatas bravas, heat a lug of olive oil in a large pan over a medium heat. Add the onion and fry for 2–3 minutes. Add the garlic, chilli and paprika and cook for 2–3 minutes. Add the wine and bring to a simmer. Add the tomatoes, tomato purée and a pinch of sugar, stir and bring to the boil. Simmer for about 10 minutes, until the sauce has thickened. Turn off the heat and set aside.

5 Now cook the chicken. Heat a lug of olive oil in a frying pan over a medium heat. Fry the chicken breasts for about 8 minutes each side (depending on thickness) until they are charred and cooked through.

6 Meanwhile, prepare the chorizo. Heat a lug of olive oil in a pan over a medium heat, add the garlic and fry for 30 seconds. Add the chorizo and fry for a few minutes. Add the red wine and bay leaves and stir well. Cook over a low heat for about 15 minutes, until the sauce has reduced, stirring regularly to ensure the chorizo doesn't burn.

7 Now prepare everything for serving. Reheat the patatas bravas sauce. When it's nice and hot, add a few drops of Tabasco, stir in the parsley and season to taste. Pour the patatas bravas sauce over the roasted potato pieces in the ovenproof dish and serve immediately. Slice the paprika chicken and arrange on a warmed serving dish. Tip the chorizo and red wine sauce into another warmed serving dish. Dig in!

PASTA WITH BUTTERNUT SQUASH, SAGE AND SMOKY BACON

Butternut squash is a gorgeous winter vegetable. In this recipe, the roasted butternut squash takes on a rich softness and blends beautifully with the pasta. This is comfort food at its best: the combination of the sweet, salty, smoky flavours and the smooth texture of the pasta is heaven on a plate. A lovely, warming dish. Serves 4

a handful of pine nuts (optional)
1 butternut squash
olive oil
salt and freshly ground black pepper
450 g farfalle or penne pasta
5 slices smoky bacon, cut into thin strips
2 tablespoons finely chopped fresh sage
butter
Parmesan, grated (optional)

1 Preheat the oven to 200°C/400°F/gas 6.

2 Toast the pine nuts, if using. Heat a small pan over a medium heat and add the pine nuts. Toast them for a few minutes, tossing regularly, until golden. Tip them into a bowl and set aside.

3 Cut the butternut squash in half lengthways and scoop out all the seeds and stringy bits. Lay the butternut halves flat side down on a chopping board and use a potato peeler to peel them. Cut the flesh into bite-sized cubes and place them in an ovenproof dish. Add a lug of olive oil, season and mix well to coat evenly. Roast for about 35 minutes, until soft and golden.

4 Cook the pasta in a large pan of boiling salted water, according to packet instructions. Always cook pasta in a large volume of water. The Italians say the water should be as salty as sea water, so use plenty of salt and you won't have to season after cooking. Cook the pasta until al dente (tender but firm to the bite). Drain the pasta, keeping back some of the cooking water. Return the pasta to its pan and stir with a few tablespoons of the cooking water. This will help to loosen the pasta and retain the seasoning.

5 Meanwhile, heat a large pan over a medium-high heat. Add the bacon and fry for about 5 minutes, until it turns crispy at the edges. Pour off any excess fat and add the sage. Fry for 30 seconds, then add the roasted butternut pieces. Stir well and cook for 2 minutes, then add the pine nuts, if using.

6 Add the hot pasta to the pan with the butternut. Add a knob of butter and as much of the pasta cooking water as you need to loosen the mixture. Stir well and season to taste.

7 Serve immediately in warmed bowls and garnish with grated Parmesan.

EASY-PEASY STICKY TOFFEE PUDDING

Sticky, gooey, soft, toffee goodness! I don't know anyone who doesn't love this pudding. It's rich, comforting and perfect for a cold winter night. I think there's a misconception that sticky toffee pudding is really difficult to make – it really isn't. This recipe is incredibly simple and must be tried to be appreciated! The delicious toffee sauce can also be used in other desserts and is particularly good poured over vanilla ice cream. **Serves 6**

200 g pitted dates, chopped
1 teaspoon bread soda (bicarbonate of soda)
250 ml weak black tea, simmering
85 g butter, softened (preferably unsalted)
70 g brown sugar
100 g caster sugar
2 eggs, lightly beaten
170 g self-raising flour
½ teaspoon mixed spice

For the toffee sauce
125 g butter, preferably unsalted
175 g brown sugar
170 ml double cream

1 Preheat the oven to 180°C/350°F/gas 4. Grease a 20 cm (8 inch) cake tin or suitable ovenproof dish.

2 Place the dates and bread soda in a bowl and pour over the tea. Leave to soak for about 10 minutes.

3 Meanwhile, cream the butter and sugars in a large bowl with an electric beater, until pale and fluffy. Gradually beat in the eggs until well combined. Sift in the flour and mixed spice. With the mixer on low, beat until fully combined.

4 Fold the date mixture into the flour mixture in the large bowl. Pour the batter into the prepared tin. Bake for 30–40 minutes, until the top is just firm.

5 Meanwhile, make the toffee sauce. Place the butter, sugar and cream in a medium pan over a low heat. Stir until the butter melts and the sugar dissolves. Simmer for about 5 minutes, until the sauce thickens and turns a lovely toffee colour.

6 To serve, divide portions of warm pudding among serving plates. Pour over the lovely toffee sauce and finish with a scoop of vanilla ice cream or a dollop of crème fraîche.

DECEMBER

CHRISTMAS IS MY ABSOLUTE FAVOURITE TIME OF YEAR. FRIENDS AND FAMILY ALL FLOCK HOME FOR A FEW WEEKS AND THERE ARE ENDLESS PARTIES AND GATHERINGS TO GO TO, WHERE YOU CAN CATCH UP AND LAUGH AWAY TOGETHER INTO THE EARLY HOURS. WHAT COULD BE BETTER? THE OTHER FANTASTIC THING ABOUT CHRISTMAS IS THAT IT'S THE ONE TIME OF YEAR THAT WE ALL ALLOW OURSELVES TO INDULGE IN AN ENORMOUS AMOUNT OF GORGEOUSLY RICH AND DELICIOUS FOOD. THERE ARE SOME LOVELY FESTIVE RECIPES IN THIS CHAPTER AND I HOPE YOU ENJOY THEM WITH YOUR NEAREST AND DEAREST.

SAUSAGES AND LENTILS WITH BABY LEAF SALAD AND HONEY MUSTARD DRESSING

This is a hearty rustic stew that turns a packet of sausages into a comforting one-pot wonder! I adore lentils and always have them in my store cupboard: they're brilliant for bulking up meals and are really inexpensive, too. Sausages and lentils go amazingly well together – the lentils absorb the richness of the sausages and allow their fantastic flavour to shine.

I'm a big fan of one-pot meals: effortless cooking and minimal washing up is just perfect, if you ask me. The simple salad is all you need on the side – and you can even leave that out, if you wish. **Serves 4**

For the dressing
2 tablespoons sunflower oil
2 tablespoons olive oil
2 tablespoons white wine vinegar
I teaspoon wholegrain mustard
I teaspoon honey

olive oil
8 thick, good-quality pork sausages, whole
I large onion, finely chopped
2 garlic cloves, crushed

4 slices pancetta or smoky bacon, diced
2 x 400 g cans chopped tomatoes
2 sprigs of rosemary
I bay leaf
125 ml red wine
$^{1}/_{2}$ teaspoon dried chilli flakes (optional)
180 g puy lentils, rinsed and drained (green or
   brown lentils also work well)
salt and freshly ground black pepper
4 handfuls of mixed baby salad leaves

1 Use a balloon whisk to mix all the ingredients for the dressing in a small bowl. Season and set aside.

2 Heat a lug of olive oil in a large pan over a high heat. Add the sausages and fry for 6–7 minutes, turning occasionally until beginning to brown all over. Remove the sausages to a plate and set aside.

3 Turn the heat to low. Add the onion and garlic to the pan and fry for about 3 minutes, until softened. Add the pancetta, increase the heat and cook for 3–4 minutes, until it has coloured and the onions are slightly singed around the edges. Add the tomatoes, rosemary, bay leaf, wine, 400 ml water and chilli, if using. Bring to the boil, then add the lentils and cooked sausages. Stir well, cover and simmer gently for 30–40 minutes, until the lentils are tender. You may need to add some boiling water throughout cooking if all the liquid is absorbed before the lentils are cooked. Be careful not to overcook the lentils or they'll lose their shape.

4 Just before serving, tip the salad leaves into a bowl and drizzle over enough of the dressing to lightly coat the leaves. Taste the stew, season if needs be and serve it straight from the pot.

CRANBERRY AND COCONUT FLORENTINES

Florentines are really elegant Italian biscuits made by setting nuts and dried fruits in caramel and coating the bases with dark chocolate. These slim, beautiful biscuits are a bit more time-consuming than other biscuits, but they look so impressive and make great gifts at Christmas time – people will think you're a genius baker!

Traditional recipes use candied peel and glacé cherries but I've gone for dried cranberry and coconut, which is a lovely combination and so Christmassy. Double the recipe if you want to make more for gifts. **Makes about 12 Florentines**

30 g butter, plus extra for greasing
70 g brown sugar
I tablespoon flour, plus extra for dusting
60 ml double cream
40 g flaked almonds

20 g blanched almonds
40 g desiccated coconut
70 g dried cranberries
150 g dark chocolate (70% cocoa solids),
  chopped

I Preheat the oven to 180°C/350°F/gas 4. Grease a few baking sheets with butter and dust them lightly with flour.

2 Melt the butter, together with the sugar and flour, in a medium pan over a low heat and keep stirring until the mixture has melted. Add the cream, stirring continuously until you have a nice, smooth caramel. Add the almonds, coconut and cranberries. Mix well to combine, then remove from the heat.

3 Place heaped teaspoonfuls of the mixture onto the baking sheets, leaving plenty of space in between. Use the back of a spoon to flatten them into thin rounds. This can be a little tricky, so use your fingers to help flatten them and don't worry if they look a little messy: they'll spread out beautifully in the oven.

4 Bake for 12 minutes, until golden brown. Remove them from the oven and leave to cool for 2–3 minutes on the baking sheets, before moving them to a wire rack to cool further. Work quickly: if you leave them too long on the baking sheets, they become hard and difficult to remove.

5 Now melt the chocolate in a heatproof bowl over a saucepan of simmering water. Make sure the bottom of the bowl doesn't touch the water. Don't stir until the chocolate is almost melted, then give it a gentle stir and remove from the heat.

6 Turn the Florentines base side up on the wire rack. Use a teaspoon to coat the base of each one with some melted chocolate. When the chocolate has almost set, use a skewer to draw a zig-zag on the Florentines.

7 Leave them to cool completely and harden. Store in an airtight container or, if you're giving them as gifts, pack them in pretty gift boxes.

CHRISTMASSY RED VELVET CUPCAKES

It's not so much the taste of these cupcakes but the look of them that makes them so Christmassy. The gorgeous, deep-red colour of the sponge alongside the snow-white cream cheese icing makes the cupcakes seem very luxurious. Perfect little Christmas treats... Makes 12 cupcakes

65 g butter, softened (preferably unsalted)
155 g caster sugar
1 large egg
1/2 teaspoon vanilla extract
1 tablespoon cocoa powder
2 tablespoons red food colouring
120 ml buttermilk, divided
150 g plain flour
1/2 teaspoon baking powder

salt
1 teaspoon white vinegar
1/2 teaspoon bread soda (bicarbonate of soda)

For the icing

300 g icing sugar, sieved
50 g butter, softened (preferably unsalted)
120 g cream cheese

1 Preheat the oven to 180°C/350°F/gas 4. Line a muffin tin with 12 paper cases.

2 Cream the butter and sugar in a large bowl with an electric beater, until pale and fluffy. Add the egg and vanilla extract and beat until combined.

3 In a small bowl, mix the cocoa powder with the food colouring to make a very thick paste. Add this paste to the butter and egg mixture, and beat well to combine. Pour in half the buttermilk and beat again until well combined.

4 Sift the flour, baking powder and a pinch of salt into another bowl. Pour half this flour mix into the batter in the large bowl and beat well. Add the remaining buttermilk and beat again. Now add the remaining flour mix and beat well for a few minutes.

5 Place the vinegar and bread soda in a small bowl and stir to combine. Add this mixture to the cake batter and beat well for a few minutes.

6 Use a spoon to divide the cake batter evenly among the baking cases, so that they are two-thirds full. Bake for 20 minutes, until springy to the touch and a skewer inserted comes out clean. Leave the cupcakes to cool in the tray for a few minutes before removing them to a wire rack.

7 Meanwhile, make the icing. Beat the icing sugar and butter in a medium bowl with an electric beater until combined. Add the cream cheese and beat again. Beat the mixture for about 5 minutes to get a really fluffy, pale icing.

8 When the cupcakes have cooled fully, dollop a spoon of icing on top of each one. Spread the icing but make sure you don't cover the cupcakes completely – the pretty red sponge must be visible.

9 You could also use a piping bag to put a pretty swirl of icing on top of each cupcake. And to make them extra festive, you could sprinkle them with some red edible glitter.

PAN-FRIED FILLET STEAK WITH SPINACH AND POTATO GRATIN

Potato gratin is a very rich and luxurious dish. With the season of indulgence now upon us, there's no better time to treat yourself with this recipe for a deliciously creamy potato and spinach gratin. Serve it with a fillet steak and it becomes a special meal to savour. **Serves 4**

4 x 200 g fillet steaks (3–4 cm thick)
I garlic clove, halved lengthways
salt and freshly ground black pepper
olive oil

For the gratin
750 g potatoes, peeled and thinly sliced (about 4 mm)
butter, for greasing
250 g spinach, washed and stalks removed (baby spinach leaves also work well)
300 ml cream

1 Preheat the oven to 180°C/350°F/gas 4. Grease a large, shallow ovenproof dish.

2 Rub each steak with the cut side of the garlic clove. Grind black pepper over both sides of the steaks, rub them with olive oil and set aside.

3 Dry the potato slices with kitchen paper. Layer half of them in the base of the ovenproof dish, allowing them to overlap a little. Season and set aside.

4 Heat a large frying pan over a medium heat and add the spinach to the dry pan. Cook until the spinach has just wilted, stirring from time to time. Remove the spinach to a plate and place another plate directly on top of the spinach. Over a sink, squeeze the plates together to remove excess water from the spinach. When the spinach is drained, roughly chop it, then layer it over the potato slices in the ovenproof dish. Season and layer the remaining potato slices on top.

5 Heat the cream in a small pan over a medium heat, until it reaches simmering point. Season and pour the cream over the potatoes. Bake for 50–60 minutes, until the gratin is golden brown and crispy on top.

6 When the gratin is almost ready, cook the steaks. Heat a grill pan or frying pan over a high heat. Sprinkle both sides of the steaks with salt and place them in the hot pan. Cook for about 4 minutes each side for medium rare (longer if you prefer). Transfer the steaks to a plate and cover with tin foil to rest for a few minutes.

7 Serve the steaks on warmed plates with a generous helping of the potato and spinach gratin.

THROW-IT-ALL-IN FRITTATA

A frittata is the Italian version of the Spanish tortilla or omelette. Frittatas are first cooked in a frying pan, then finished under the grill so that the top becomes lovely and golden. They're one of the simplest, quickest and most economical meals you can make – not to mention how delicious they are.

If you have any leftover vegetables or meat in the fridge, frittatas are a great way to use them up. You just throw them all in a pan, add a few eggs and the result is epic!

This recipe includes those ingredients I always have to hand: eggs, onions, bacon, mushrooms, spinach and cherry tomatoes. How could you go wrong? **Serves 2–4**

olive oil
5–6 slices bacon, chopped
1 onion, thinly sliced
150 g button mushrooms, sliced
salt and freshly ground black pepper
100 g baby spinach leaves
a handful of cherry tomatoes, halved
4 tablespoons chopped fresh parsley
6 large eggs, lightly beaten and seasoned

1 Preheat your grill to a high heat.

2 Heat a little olive oil in a large, ovenproof frying pan over a medium-high heat. Fry the bacon until lightly browned and crisp. Use a slotted spoon to remove the bacon from the pan and drain on kitchen paper on a warm plate.

3 Add the onion to the pan and fry until softened. Add the mushrooms, season, and fry for about 3 minutes, until the mushrooms release their juices. Add the spinach and cook until it wilts. Stir in the tomatoes and parsley.

4 Return the bacon to the pan, stirring well. Spread out the contents of the pan, then pour in the eggs. Use a wooden spoon to move the ingredients around, so that the eggs leak into any available gaps.

5 Cook for a few minutes, then use a spatula to lift the edge of the frittata to check that it is softly set and golden underneath. Place the pan under the hot grill and cook until it turns golden brown and is just set on top. Don't overcook it: it's best when still a little soft in the centre.

6 Cut the frittata into slices and serve on warmed plates with some nice, crusty bread on the side.

JESSIE'S GOOEY HOT CHOC PUD

This self-saucing chocolate pudding is one that my cousin Jessie made for me years ago and I've kept her hand-written recipe safely ever since! It's an absolute dream for chocolate lovers. The sponge mix is covered with sauce before baking, which results in an incredibly moist, gooey, saucy chocolate pudding.

The recipe calls for an ovenproof dish of 1.5–2 litre capacity. Sometimes I make one big pudding in a dish of about 25 cm (10 inches) diameter. I've also divided the mixture into smaller bowls to make individual puddings, which are so cute. I root out this recipe every winter and it impresses me every time! Thank you, Jessie x
Serves 4–6

75 g self-raising flour
2 tablespoons cocoa powder
salt
110 g butter, plus extra for greasing
110 g caster sugar
2 eggs, mixed with 1 teaspoon vanilla extract

For the sauce
110 g brown sugar
2 tablespoons cocoa powder
300 ml boiling water

1 Preheat the oven to 180°C/350°F/gas 4. Grease an ovenproof dish (or several dishes, for smaller puddings).

2 Sift the flour, cocoa and a pinch of salt into a bowl and set aside.

3 Cream the butter and sugar in a large bowl with an electric beater, until pale and fluffy. Add in most of the egg and vanilla mixture, beating well to combine. Add the remainder of the egg and vanilla mixture, along with a small amount of the flour mixture, and beat well. Gradually add the rest of the flour mixture, beating well after each addition, until fully incorporated. Pour the batter into the ovenproof dish and set aside while you make the sauce.

4 Place the sugar, cocoa and boiling water in a heatproof bowl. Stir until the sugar dissolves. Pour this liquid over the batter in the ovenproof dish. Bake for 40 minutes, until the sponge has risen and the sauce bubbles up around the sides. (Individual puddings in smaller bowls take just 25–30 minutes.)

5 Serve with a dollop of crème fraîche or a scoop of vanilla ice cream on top.

HONEY-ROASTED DUCK WITH CREAMY PARSNIPS AND GRAVY

Christmas isn't all about turkey! It's nice to try alternative festive meals throughout the holiday season. Duck is full of flavour and much easier to cook than a big bird – a great option if you're cooking for a small group of people. You could serve this dish with some roast potatoes. Serves 2–4

1 duck, weighing 1.8–2 kg
salt and freshly ground black pepper
2 bay leaves
2 garlic cloves, unpeeled
a few sprigs of thyme
6 tablespoons honey, for basting
125 ml red wine

300 ml chicken stock, simmering

For the parsnips
duck stock (optional)
4 large parsnips, peeled and chopped
60 ml cream

1 Preheat the oven to 220°C/425°F/gas 7.

2 Dry the outside of the duck with kitchen paper and season inside and out. Using a skewer, lightly prick the skin where it's most fatty, being careful not to pierce the flesh. This ensures that, when roasted, the duck fat will run but the meat will retain its lovely juices. Place the bay leaves, garlic and thyme into the cavity and place the duck on a wire rack over a roasting tray.

3 Roast the duck in the hot oven for 10 minutes, then reduce the heat to 180°C/350°F/gas 4 and roast for a further 50–60 minutes.

4 Meanwhile, prepare the parsnips. Place the parsnips in a large pan of boiling water (or duck stock, if using). Cook for 15–20 minutes, until tender. Drain, reserving a few tablespoons of the cooking water. Tip the cooked parsnips and a little cooking water into a food processor. Blitz to make a smooth purée. Add the cream, season and blitz again until combined. Keep the parsnips warm until serving.

5 The duck will need to be basted during the final 30 minutes of roasting. Remove it from the oven every 5 minutes or so and spread about a tablespoon of honey all over the duck. (Make sure you close the oven door while basting, so no heat escapes!)

6 After 50 minutes of roasting, insert a skewer into the thickest part of the duck leg. If the juices run clear, it's done; if the juices are still pink, return the duck to the oven for another 10 minutes. Once the duck is cooked, tilt it to release any juices from inside the cavity into the roasting tray. Remove the duck to a warm plate, cover with foil and leave to rest.

7 Now make the gravy. Remove the wire rack from the roasting tray. Carefully pour off any fat from the tray into a heatproof bowl, leaving the brown juices in the tray. Place the tray on the hob over a medium heat. Add the red wine, simmer and scrape the bottom of the tray to release all the nice caramelised bits. Add the stock and simmer until it reduces into a rich gravy. Season to taste, then strain through a sieve into a serving jug.

8 Carve the duck and divide the meat among warmed serving plates, alongside the creamy parsnips and gravy.

GUARD'S PUDDING

In my family, we seldom have Christmas pudding as our Christmas Day dessert. The tradition has been to have this Guard's Pudding instead; and I've yet to find a steamed pudding I prefer.

It's a really simple pudding made mainly with breadcrumbs and raspberry jam, then steamed for a few hours. The result is a moist, incredibly moreish dessert. I have several helpings of it every Christmas Day, before collapsing in a post-Christmas-dinner heap on the sofa. But isn't that what Christmas Day is all about? **Makes 1 pudding**

150 g white breadcrumbs
1 level teaspoon bread soda (bicarbonate of soda), mixed with a few drops of water
75 g caster sugar
75 g butter, melted, plus extra for greasing
3 eggs, beaten
5 rounded tablespoons raspberry jam

1 Grease a 1 litre pudding bowl.

2 Place all the ingredients in a food processor and blitz until smooth. Pour the mixture into the pudding bowl and seal with a lid. (If you don't have a lid, loosely cover the bowl with tin foil or greaseproof paper, then secure it with a piece of string, so that it is well sealed.)

3 Place the pudding bowl in a large saucepan and pour in boiling water to come half-way up the sides of the pudding bowl. Cover the saucepan with a lid and simmer for 2 hours, checking it now and then and topping up with boiling water if needs be. (Do not let the pan boil dry.)

4 Turn out the pudding and serve with lots of cream or crème fraîche. Delish!

INDEX

RECIPE INDEX BY COURSES

DESSERTS

BAKED TREATS

SOPHIE MORRIS is an energetic 28 year old and owner of the innovative and exciting young Irish food company Kooky Dough. Started in her kitchen and initially selling at farmers' markets in Dublin, Sophie and her business partner, Graham Clarke, famously turned down the dragons on RTÉ's 'Dragons' Den' to build their food business their own way. Kooky Dough is now stocked in supermarkets and premium independent retailers in Ireland; in Waitrose in the UK; in Monoprix in France; and in Spinneys in the United Arab Emirates. Kooky Dough and Sophie have received extensive recognition for the quality of their product by winning numerous Blas na hÉireann food awards in Ireland, and Gold in the UK's Great Taste Awards 2011.

With an MSc distinction in Economics along with a degree in Economics and Social Studies from Trinity College Dublin, Sophie enjoyed the challenge of academia and was always drawn to business oriented subjects. However, away from the lecture halls Sophie developed an intense passion for food, not only in the eating but in the therapy of preparing and cooking. She completed an Italian cookery course in Rome in 2007, and after university she completed the 12-week Ballymaloe cookery course to develop her culinary skills further. Her experiences at Ballymaloe only heightened her love for food and it was here that she developed the ambition to have her own food business.

Cooking simple, feelgood food is what Sophie loves to do in her precious free time; it helps her to relax and escape from work. She hopes this book will help you to do the same.